NO BACKUP NEEDED

Veteran New York City Cops Struggle Through
The Summer Of 1975
(The Year New York City Went Bust)

JAMES J. KAVANAUGH

RED ANVIL PRESS

Our books are available from your favorite bookstore, amazon.com, or from our
24 hour order line: 1.800.431.1579

Library of Congress Control Number: 2010940069
Publisher's Catalog-in-Publication Data
No Backup Needed / James J. Kavanaugh
ISBN-13: 978-1-934956-36-6
ISBN-10: 1934956368
1. Cops—Fiction.
2. NYPD—Fiction.
3. Police—Fiction.
4. NYC—Fiction.
5. True Crime—Fiction.
I. Title

This book was written, printed and bound in the United States of America.

WARNING!!!!

Liberals reading this book may experience high blood pressure, nervous tics, hives, or a mild outbreak of logical thinking. If your symptoms last longer than four hours, affected readers are advised to watch CNN or MSNBC until your condition improves.

This story is written in raw *cop talk*, without the moral timidity of political correctness. I apologize to any ethnic group that I have failed to offend in this book. There's always the chance of offending you in the sequel.

This book is dedicated to my brother 'Frank.'
May God grant you the happiness in the next life
that was taken from you in this one.

Contents

Author's Note

As a rookie cop in the New York City Police Department I worked in the old Greenwich Village station house on Charles Street that was built in 1896. The bronze plaque on the wall opposite the Lieutenant's desk read:
"THEODORE ROOSEVELT—POLICE COMMISSIONER."

Although I was just a working class kid, I realized that I was part of a very fine organization with a great history, and I was proud to be a member of it.

I owe a great deal to my friend, retired NYPD Lieutenant, Patrick Picciarelli, for his advice and guidance. Pat is a distinguished author who has published several works, including the hilarious book *Jimmy The Wags.*

Another person who helped me greatly and encouraged me along the way is my friend from the United States Army Military Police Corps, Charles "Chuck" Kelly. It was Chuck who came up with the title for the book. He is also a noted author of mystery novels. His latest book is entitled *Pay Here,* a riveting murder mystery novel set in the southwest.

This book is a fictional characterization about events taking place in New York City, in and about the summer of 1975. All of the characters in this book are fictional. Any similarity between any character portrayed in this book, and any person, living or deceased, is purely coincidental.

Foreword

The name's Jimmy Kavanaugh, now a retired Lieutenant from the New York City Police Department. Although I am telling this story about the events of the summer of 1975, the story is not so much about me and my partner, Tommy McInerney, but about the great cops who held the City of New York together in a time of fiscal and social crisis. In 1964, I joined the NYPD right out of high school as a Police Trainee. After going through the Police Academy, I worked at administrative jobs in headquarters and field commands. At age twenty-one, they gave me a gun and a shield, and sent me to patrol the streets of Greenwich Village.

After one year as a Police Officer, Uncle Sam came calling and I wound up in the Military Police Corps for two years. Upon being discharged, I came right back to the 6th Precinct in the old Charles Street station house, as if I had never left. The NYPD was like a family to me, and it always will be, to my dying days.

All was going great in my life until the spring of 1975, when the City of New York went broke, and my life took what I first thought was a downward spiral, but was really a free-fall into an abyss of financial distress and personal crisis. The following is a fictional account of life in Manhattan's 13th Precinct, in that long ago summer of 1975.

ADIOS, POLICE ACADEMY

The early days of spring, 1975 were a blessing. Winter had been cold, damp and dreary, with heavy snowfalls and nasty, icy weather. The muster deck on the third floor of the New York City Police Academy was made out of faded black tile, and the off-white brick of the parapet clashed with the deck. Now, with the warm weather, the Police Academy staff could conduct their morning roll call outdoors on the deck.

The instructors were, as usual, in dress uniforms, with blue summer blouses and white shirts. The recruits were now in their dress blue uniforms with light blue shirts. Final exams were completed, and all of my students passed. Only one of my guys dropped out, a Chinese kid from Elizabeth Street, in Chinatown. For the most part, my recruits were gung-ho Vietnam era veterans, and were going to make great street cops.

Although they had passed the recruit school, there would be no letdown in discipline among the students. Roll call was conducted by the company sergeants, with the official instructors supervising. There was a nervous, almost giddy behavior among the troops, because they did not know where they were going after graduation.

I recalled being a raw recruit on this same muster deck, nearly eleven years before, and how young and naïve I was. My idealism had tarnished, just like the worn out tiles of the muster deck, and the once alabaster colored bricks of the parapet.. At age twenty-nine I felt that I had seen and done it all, and nobody could tell me otherwise.

This was Friday morning, and assignments would be given out this afternoon, with the official graduation ceremony being on Monday. A sense of uneasiness permeated throughout the staff, however. There had been rumors of the pending financial collapse of the City of New York, and closing of the Police Academy. Frankly, I thought it was total nonsense. How could a major American city just go broke? This was Friday, and I was teaching a class of tactics from 8 A.M. to Noon. Then it was off to lunch at the Honey Tree for me.

The Honey Tree was a great place for lunch, with Harry the bartender's jokes and antics. He spoke with an Italian accent, and whenever Harry would mention his ex-wife, Maria, he would reflexively say *miserab'*. This woman must have been the meanest bitch in Brooklyn.

On the way out to lunch, my boss, Sgt. Jack Drumm, told me that the Chief was having a staff meeting at 3:00 P.M. Attendance was mandatory for all. What a way to ruin a weekend! Lunch was uneventful, as the guys at my table discussed the layoff rumors that had been floating around for the past week. At 3:00 P.M. the entire staff of about fifty men and women was assembled in the master conference room on the fifth floor.

Chief Willem Van Der Steig, the Commanding Officer of the Police Academy, stood solemnly at the podium in the front of the room. The Chief wore a dark blue, three piece, pinstripe suit and a red tie, which bespoke his inner anger. He tried to be the Hollywood image of a New York City Police Chief, and succeeded, somewhat, with his lean six foot frame, buzz cut reddish-gray hair, and military rigidity.

To his right sat his loyal lackey and obsequious sycophant, Captain Hugh McGuinness, his wife's cousin. Capt. McGuinness had been Van Der Steig's personal toady for many years. The man didn't have the balls of a field mouse, having been neutered by Van Der Steig long ago when he was a Sergeant and the Chief was a Captain. His pale, pasty face gave an indication of having low blood pressure, and the twenty or thirty strands of brown hair that he had left were combed over his scalp, and matted down with

11

a Bryllcream-like substance. He wore a brown tweed jacket with leather elbows, and smoked a pipe non-stop, which he felt made him look scholarly. In reality, the man was a buffoon with a G.E.D. diploma, in way over his head, and he didn't have a fucking clue.

Earlier in his career, Chief Van Der Steig was once a beer drinking guy from Brooklyn. Then the NYPD sent him to Yale for six months for a management course. He came back as an aristocratic, dry balls, chablis sipping, brie eating snob. He was now an insufferable, miserable, elitist WASP. Van Der Steig treated his staff terribly, but kissed the recruits' asses so much that it made maintaining discipline difficult for the instructors.

Yet, this was the best job I ever had, teaching in the New York City Police Academy, and I was damn proud of it.

The first item on the agenda was "minority retention." After his stint at Yale, Van Der Steig came back as a man anally obsessed with "minority recruitment and retention."

Whenever a minority quit or failed out of the Academy, Van Der Steig would go ballistic, trying to find out what went wrong.

In the last month only one minority quit. He was my recruit, a Chinese kid named Jimmy Huw, from Elizabeth Street in Chinatown. He really didn't quit, but was picked up as a deep undercover by the Intelligence Division. I saw them interviewing him in a diner around the corner from the Academy. It must have been pretty secret if they didn't even tell the Chief. I knew all about Huw, but kept quiet about it.

Van Der Steig was breathing fire when he asked those assembled "Why did the Oriental recruit quit?"

Nobody answered, and he asked again "I want a goddam answer, now!"

He barked again at the gelded one, Captain McGuinness:

"McGuinness, Huw quit, why did he?"

In an Abbott and Costello-like routine, McGuinness said. "Who quit, Chief?"

"Yes, Captain, I know Huw quit, and I want to know why."

12

Before the deballed Captain could say "I don't know who quit," and prolong the unintended comedy act, the Chief then looked menacingly at Captain No Balls and said "McGuiness, who is Probationary Officer Huw's official company instructor?"

The Captain nervously pointed to me and said "It's Kavanaugh, Chief."

"Kavanaugh, why did the Oriental recruit quit?", barked out Van Der Steig, with his intimidating, bushy gray eyebrows glowering down at me .

"I really don't know, Chief. He didn't tell me why he left."

"That's not good enough for me, officer, I want an answer, right here and now, why did this Oriental recruit quit?"

Put me on the spot, you WASP bastard? "Well, Chief, I guess he just didn't have a *yen* for police work."

The room roared with laughter. Even McGuinness looked nervously at the Chief to see if he were allowed to laugh. He got his answer immediately as Van Der Steig's face turned purple with rage, and the veins in his neck popped out. I knew that my career in the Police Academy just came to a screeching halt. I just didn't grasp how quickly it was going to end, nor did I particularly give a damn by now.

Realizing his exalted position, the Chief regained his composure and went into the next topic. "Ladies and gentlemen, Police Commissioner Michael Codd, and Mayor Abraham Beame, have informed the leadership of the NYPD that there will be no more hiring of police officers in this city, at least until the next fiscal year. Therefore, there will be no need for a Police Academy staff. Beginning today, some members of the Police Academy staff will be transferred back to patrol.

"Captain McGuinness has the roster of personnel who will be going to field commands, as of tomorrow. "

At first, I was not on the list. However, I was soon to learn that the first name on the list was crossed off, and my name was inserted by the Chief.

"Fuck you, *Van Der Schmuck*, you pompous ass!" I said to myself.

I was notified that I would be going to the 13th Precinct on East 21st Street. It was even in the same building as the Academy, just that the entrance was on 21st Street, instead of 20th Street. No problem here. I just carried my locker downstairs, with the help of a friend, Pat Panarico. Pat was a former paratrooper from Vietnam with multiple Purple Hearts, three Bronze Stars and a Silver Star. He was going to the 24th Precinct on the upper west side of Manhattan, and he didn't give a damn, either.

WELCOME TO THE 13TH PRECINCT

I hesitated to call my wife, Mary Ann. She was a nurse and we both had weekends off, and my new assignment would severely disrupt our social life. Finally, I called and said "It's me, honey. The City is going broke, and they just dumped a bunch of us from the Academy. I'm going back to patrol, along with about thirty-five other guys."

Mary Ann was upset. "Where are you going?"

"They sent me to the 13th Precinct on East 21st Street. It's not a bad place."

My wife knew a lot about the area and said "Isn't that the neighborhood with all of the Irish and German bars, where we go out sometimes?"

I replied "Yeah, you know it well. Rolf's, Molly Malone's, the Gloccamorra, the Anawanda Club, and the Abbey Tavern."

My wife was skeptical, and said. "Jimmy, sending you there is like putting a diabetic in a candy factory. You like to drink too much."

It was an astute observation. Alcoholism didn't just run in my Irish-German family, it galloped. I had uncles who were refused cremation, because the funeral director thought it would take a week or more to put the fire out.

My family's track record with drinking was not an enviable one, to say the least. I guess, due to genetics, I had a taste for beer, and had to be careful not to go overboard with the sauce.

About half an hour after getting axed from the Academy, I stopped by the 13th Precinct roll call office to introduce myself. The roll call man was an old timer named Police Officer Jake Levinsky,

15

a jovial man in his mid fifties with a rum blossom, W.C. Fields-like nose, with beer, mustard, and ketchup stains on his uniform tie.

"I'm Police Officer Jimmy Kavanaugh, just transferred to the 13th from the Police Academy. I'm not a rookie. I was on the staff and lost my detail after a run-in with the Chief."

What better way to introduce yourself, but as a guy who locked horns with a boss?

Levinsky sized me up and asked "How much time ya' got on the job, kid?"

Somehow, I didn't mind being called *kid* by this man, since he had a very pleasant way about him. He meant no disrespect, nor did I suspect that he did.

"I'll have eleven years on in July."

Levinsky said "Well, Jimmy, I guess that you worked all week, and your R.D.O's (regular days off) are Saturday and Sunday. Tell you what, you can go into the 9th Squad, and they have Monday and Tuesday off. So, get yourself a locker, and report in for the 4 to 12 shift on Wednesday.

"By the way, here's a list of the guys in the squad. Who do you want to work with?"

I looked over the roster and saw a familiar name. It was Ben Harrigan, who was one of my students who graduated the past October. He was a decent young guy, so I thought that he would be a good patrol partner.

Wanting to repay the roll call man for my two extra days off, on the way out I said "Jake, you look a little dry, are you in need of a taste?"

"My liver's beech wood aged, kid" was the response, and the *square bag* of Budweiser was brought in for him in about five minutes.

My first week on patrol was great. I was reunited with Ben and we were a good team. Harrigan was a good looking Irish kid, only twenty-one years old, about five feet, ten inches tall. He had jet black hair, and needed to shave only three times a week. Ben

16

lived in Bay Ridge, Brooklyn with his widowed mother, Kathleen. This kid loved being a cop, so I didn't let my cynicism tarnish his idealistic view of "the job."

In the past six months, Ben had learned nearly nothing. There was a clique of Long Islanders who shunned other cops who lived in the New York City limits. They looked down on us as if we were untouchables, like those poor bastards in India. The clique members hardly ever spoke to cops outside of their own group. They had frozen young Ben out and taught him nothing. The Long Island guys kept mainly to themselves, and shunned the other cops in the Precinct.

Typical was the radio car crew of Louis Mazzarella and Brian Conner, sector 13 Charlie. They stayed within their own group and had little to do with the rest of us. As events unfolded, we would become involved with them, very soon.

NO BACK-UP NEEDED

The dispatcher called 13 Charlie, manned by Mazzarella and Conner, to send them to an assault in progress in apartment 3C, 264 3rd Avenue. I said to Ben "That's just a few blocks away, let's back them up."

We arrived at the same time as the other sector, outside of the five story, red brick tenement building. Arriving on the scene, macho man Conner, all 5', 8" and 140 pounds of him, blurted out "What the fuck are you doing here?"

I told him "We're here for your back-up."

With a sense of swagger, Conner replied "I don't need a back-up. If I want a fuckin' back-up, I'll call for a fuckin' back-up. Ya' got it? No back-up needed!"

I knew enough not to publicly argue with a jerk like this, so we got back into our radio car and took off. It would be a cold day in hell before I ever help these two out, or so I thought.

As soon as we pulled out of the block, the dispatcher sent us to E. 14th Street and 2nd Avenue, for a man bleeding. That was one hell-hole of an intersection back in the seventies. Young Ben was not prepared for what we saw. A junkie had been in a donut shop and argued with another addict. He was stabbed in the neck, right in the carotid artery. Every time his heart beat, blood would spurt across 14th Street, while dozens of methadone addicts and junkies looked on in their mind-numbing stupors.

I asked the owner of the store for a towel and pressed it right over the wound, all the while wondering why I was trying to save this worthless piece of debris. The ambulance driver was an old timer who drove up First Avenue, passing Beth Israel Hospital and Carbrini Medical Center. There was no better place to take a seriously wounded person than to Bellevue Hospital. It was the crème de la crème of medical facilities. Among patrol cops it was understood that if you ever got seriously injured, you would be taken to Bellevue.

Leaving the hospital, Harrigan asked me if the guy would live. I advised him that an old timer told me many years before that street people were made out of rubber. You just can't kill them. Sure enough, a week later, this junkie would be back on the corner, shucking and jiving with his peers, with a small bandage on his neck.

Easing out of the Bellevue complex at E. 26th Street and First Avenue, I heard a faint but familiar voice coming over the radio. The voice was panicked and it was Conner in Sector Charlie, frantically calling for help. Because of the tall buildings, the signal from his hand held walkie-talkie was too weak to be picked up downtown by the dispatcher or by other radio cars in the 13th and surrounding Precincts. I picked up the radio mike and did not wait for recognition from the dispatcher, yelling out "In the 13th Precinct, signal 10-13 (assist Police Officer), called over the air by 13 Charlie. 13 Adam-Boy is responding."

Whenever any street cop worth his salt hears the call of a "10-13", it makes his balls tighten up and his asshole pucker, especially when called over the air by a fellow cop.

The veteran dispatcher pulled up 13 Charlie's job on his screen and repeated the message to all units to go to 264 Third Avenue, apartment 3C, to assist sector Charlie. I quickly realized that we were only two blocks away. No good cop would refuse to roll on a 10-13, even though it was to help two jack-offs like Mazzarella and Conner.

With the roof lights blazing, and siren wailing, we arrived in seconds. After running up the dingy wooden stairs, Ben kicked the door open, and there before us was a tremendous brawl. The once neat, working class apartment was now a shambles. The décor was early Puerto Rican: an imitation leather couch, a velvet Elvis, and pictures of Jesus and the Pope. There, fighting for their lives, were our two brave heroes, Mazzarella and Conner, the radio car crew who needed no back-up.

Jaime Hernandez , the apartment resident, died while sitting at his kitchen table. Instead of calling the police, his wife called her friends and neighbors. They had a real big party going on, with wild binge drinking. After a while, the party deteriorated into a diatribe against the deceased. "He owed me money, that son of a bitch. How am I going to get paid now?"

"He was fucking my wife" was heard from a cuckolded husband.

Soon, all involved were kicking the crap out of each other, and a neighbor called 911. It was like the Spanish version of *Tim Finnegan's Wake.* 13 Charlie, who needed no back-up, tried to handle everything. They had it under control for about 20 minutes or so, until Mazzarella, a serial womanizer, tried putting the make on one of the women. Then the shit hit the fan, and it was now the two cops against everybody else.

I chuckled a bit upon seeing the situation, until I realized that we were all going to get killed if we didn't start hurting these guys. Conner had been blindsided by being hit in the head with a frying pan, and he went down on the kitchen floor. He was semi-conscious, and was rolling around the shiny green linoleum floor like a turtle on its back. Two guys were doing the Mexican Hat Dance on him.

Mazzarella was standing on the back of the couch in the living room, swinging his nightstick like Davey Crockett on the ramparts of the Alamo. Five drunken men were throwing beer bottles and lamps at him, and the women were hitting him with brooms and mops. He was parrying the blows from the brooms and mops, and ducking the thrown objects like some carnival geek having baseballs thrown at his head.

I learned a long time ago never to hit my opponent in the head. Always go for the shins, the kneecaps, or the balls. Even the biggest guy can't grow muscles there. I had given this advice to Ben, and he was a good student. Back in the kitchen, the immediate problem was to help the injured Conner, who was bleeding badly from a head wound. Just as one man hauled off to hit Ben with a right cross, he ducked and whipped vicious blows to the man's shins. The guy rolled around the floor, groaning in pain.

Conner's other attacker met a similar fate. I faked a blow to his head. When he covered up, I gave him the butt end of my cocabola stick right square in the balls. The fool lay on the linoleum floor, holding his crotch, babbling in Spanish for *Mommy.*

Having made the world safer for Conner, it was time to relieve the *swordsman,* Mazzarella, who was not doing well in his defense of the couch. I learned a great move in the Military Police Corps: Come up behind a belligerent man, and put your nightstick between his legs. Then turn the stick so that it is parallel to the floor, and lift up. The man will tip-toe like he is filled with helium; then you can pick him up and slam him down. This worked like a charm and now it was three against four, with half a dozen drunken women cheering their men on.

Ben hit one attacker on the back of the thighs, which caused no injury, just a wicked stinging sensation. When the man turned around, Ben smashed him in the solar plexus with the tip of his stick, causing the man to puke his rum soaked guts up all over the living room carpet.

Mazzarella engaged the ringleader and gave him a head shot that knocked the guy senseless. It was what cops call a "wood shampoo". The man folded like a cheap tent. As the Book of Cynical Proverbs says, "Payback's a bitch."

Meanwhile, Conner recovered somewhat and put a towel on his head to stop the bleeding. While the battle raged on in the living room, Conner stood behind the corpse and lifted up the body. He came into the living room hiding behind the dead man shouting "Mira! Mira! Que pasa?" (Look! Look! What's happening?) The drunks began screaming, and some wet their pants upon seeing

Jaime walking around, like a latter-day Lazarus. They had to be calmed down enough just to get handcuffed.

Conner went to the hospital for stitches, and Mazzarella took the collars. We waited for the Medical Examiner to come. Of course, the D.O.A. was put back at the kitchen table, propped up, just as he was when the cops first came in.

Ben asked the deceased's wife if she knew what her husband had died from. She replied "Yeah, my man had *the roaches* for a few years."

"Pardon me, Mrs. Hernandez, but did you say he had '*the roaches?*'" "Yeah, officuh, dat's right, he died from *the roaches*. You never heard of *the roaches of the liver?* The doctor said that he got it from drinking too much."

Now, I'd heard of cirrhosis of the liver, but never *the roaches of the liver*. You just can't make this stuff up.

The next day Louis Mazzarella approached me in the locker room and apologized for him and his partner being such boorish jerks. He acknowledged that they would have been beaten senseless had we not shown up to assist them. We had a good laugh at Conner's dead man walking act, shook hands, and left it at that. Still, there was something quite odd about the whole thing. There were at least four other units available, plus two sergeants. Why the hell didn't anyone else show up? This was a 10-13 called over air by two cops who needed help. What the hell was going on in this Precinct?

I got my answer from Harrigan. He told me that the Long Island cops did not answer the radio during the last half hour of the shift, even to help each other, so they wouldn't miss their car pools. This was incredible. They thought more of their rides home than of their fellow cops' safety. This bullshit was going to change, and real soon.

22

JIMMY'S NEMESES

I wondered why the patrol supervisors, our Sergeants, didn't jack-up these lazy bastards, until I realized that they were in the same car pools. There were some damn good Sergeants, like Johnny Byrne, who made you proud to be a cop. Sgt. Byrne knew that I was a veteran cop, and treated me like one. Consequently, I never did anything that would cause Sgt. Byrne any trouble or embarrassment.

Another great boss was Sgt. Patrick "Paddy" O'Shea. Paddy was a bachelor in his mid fifties. Like many Irish immigrant families, upon arriving in America, the father and the oldest son would work hard to make sure that the younger children received an education. In the O'Shea family, the father, Dairmid, worked as a laborer, and Paddy became a cop. They were able to put the younger sons, Sean and Brian, through medical school and law school. Although the two younger boys were now professionals, Paddy was the one who was most revered in the family, because he was a New York City Police Sergeant.

Sgt. O'Shea loved to use an old line that Irish Sergeants from two or three generations ago used to use. If a cop gave Paddy a hard time, he's jokingly say with his thick brogue, "I've come three thousand miles to be your boss, and your boss I'll be."

There were some Sergeants who were real losers, like William "Wild Bill" Hanley. He was a slightly built alcoholic, missing half of his teeth. When loaded, he was an obnoxious drunk; when sober, he was a nasty dry-drunk. Hanley had a well deserved inferiority complex, since he was actually inferior to most people he met. He had passed the difficult Sergeant's test by some miracle, and wound up in the 13th Pct. Hanley could turn the simplest assignment into a massive *clusterfuck*. I disliked him, and the feeling was mutual. I felt that it was just a matter of time before he would be sent upstate to "The Farm," the place where alcoholic cops were sent to dry out.

Sgt. Kieran McNally was another problem drinker. He was just a mean-spirited man, who took his personal problems out on his subordinates. His wife, Irene, died of cancer ten years before at the age of 36, leaving McNally with four children, ages four to ten. Kieran turned to drink when he could not cope any more. Although he had his mother-in-law to help out, he was overwhelmed being a single parent. Had he not been such an abusive, nasty drunk, you could almost feel sorry for him.

I knew that it would be inevitable that we would lock horns, sooner or later. It turned out to be sooner.

JUNE 30, 1975
A DAY THAT WILL LIVE IN INFAMY

Ben and I hit if off well and became a good radio car team, as well as good friends. Throughout the early months of 1975 there had been rumors of impending layoff of police officers. Even I had to fill out some forms to prove veteran's status and prior city service to claim extra seniority, to avoid being laid off.

I saw Ben Harrigan as fair game for the layoffs, and it was a shame. A city that wasted so much money on drug addicts, phony poverty programs, welfare recipients, and just plain lazy people, did not have enough money for its own protectors. The problem with New York City was that it had too many leeches, and not enough taxpayers. Productive people in New York City were turned into sort of worker ants, used to keep the welfare colony of drones going.

The last day of June ended the City of New York's fiscal year. June 30, 1975 would be a black day for the NYPD. We were working the 4 x 12 shift. At roll call, we heard the staccato, rat-a-tat sound of the teletype printing out the names of those members of the department who would be laid off at midnight. Ben and I didn't talk about it throughout the whole shift.

Around 10:30 P.M. we found ourselves in the middle of the Precinct, having rescued someone trapped in an elevator in the Flatiron Building at 23rd and Broadway. Right after giving the disposition to the dispatcher, we were sent to 140 West 17th Street, to a burglary run. We were there in minutes, and were met in front of the tenement by a well dressed black man with a heavy Spanish accent, who recently arrived in America from Cuba. He explained that he left his apartment for a few minutes to buy cigarettes, and when he came back, his apartment was ransacked and property was stolen.

This was obviously an inside job, done by someone who knew he was not home. I asked him if anyone was around the front of the building when he left, and he replied that there were some boys sitting on the stoop who cursed at him in Spanish, and called him a "*maricon*" (homosexual).

I then asked the complainant "Are you the only black person living in this building?"

As soon as he said "yes", we raced to the back of the building, just in time to find our two burglars climbing down a tree, holding the victim's valuables in a pillow case. Caught like two treed raccoons! These were the same punks who had cursed out the complainant. They had climbed up the tree, did a trapeze move to enter the apartment, stole some property, then came back for more. I figured that since the victim was the only black person living in the building, the kids knew when he was gone, and when he was at home.

After being thanked profusely by the victim, we took our two amateur burglars to the Precinct for booking. When the Paddy Wagon came to take our prisoners to court, it was about five minutes before midnight. Captain Dan Fitzgerald, a mild mannered World War II veteran, called Ben and me into his office and congratulated us on the good collar. Then, with tears welling in his eyes, he informed Ben that he was being laid off, and asked him to turn over his shield and gun. The clinking sound of Ben's shield hitting the Captain's desk is one I will never forget for the rest of my life. It represented the utter failure of the fools who drove New York City into financial ruin.

To civilians, the police officer's shield is just a piece of metal. To a cop it is his personal symbol of honor, and to be stripped of it is a traumatic experience. Incredibly, our politicians had spent the city into near bankruptcy, leaving no money for its police. I never thought it could happen. Well, they also said the Titanic would never sink.

Ben was hired in 1974 and was one of the first to be let go. However, the list went as far back as 1968 in seniority. Cops were laid off by the thousands, and the city's seventy-five precincts would be grossly undermanned. Of the nineteen cops who worked on patrol that evening, ten of them were laid off at midnight. In addition, every female Police Officer in the Precinct was terminated.

Since I had to go to court in the morning to arraign my prisoners, there was no sense in driving home to Staten Island. I'd have a couple of beers at the Anawanda Club, and then hit the Precinct dormitory until the morning.

What the hell was wrong with New York City? Four decades of idealistic, knee-jerk liberalism had turned my home town into a city with a big heart and a small brain.

And, to top it all off, my wife was informed that she would have her days reduced at the hospital from five a week to two. I realized that I was going to be strangled slowly, in the financial sense, and my life was going to change for the worse.

JULY 1, 1975
OLD TIMERS DAY

Roll call for the day shift on July 1st consisted of a disparate cast of characters. About a dozen new faces appeared, all from cushy details like the Harbor Precinct, Aviation Unit, Public Morals, Warrant Squad, Building Maintenance, Highway Patrol, and the Detective Bureau, just to name a few. The mood was somber, and the newly transferred men were not happy about leaving their nice jobs and going back on patrol. They were a platoon of strangers for the time being, haphazardly being thrown together to protect the City of New York. It looked like a modern day *Volkssturm*.

The Sergeant turning out the platoon was an egotistical Norwegian from Bay Ridge named Sven Nordstrom. He fancied himself as some sort of Norse god, and they called him "The Viking." He was a bodybuilder who stood about six feet, two inches tall, and had a handsome, chiseled face and blonde hair. Nordstrom was such a womanizer that the Precinct joke was that he's screw a rattlesnake if he could figure out how to keep it from biting him. The last thing that these veteran cops needed was this obnoxious boss rubbing salt in their open wounds.

I was always 'spit and polish' with my uniform, a throwback to my days in the Military Police Corps, so Nordstrom never bothered me. He was a guy to stay away from, however. This morning, Sgt. Nordstrom was out to have some fun at the expense of the veterans who had been sent back to patrol, most of them on short notice.

The first one to get chewed out was Police Officer Sean Dennihy, of Highway Patrol Unit No. 1. He wore his Motorcycle Division uniform of jodhpurs, with light blue stripe, knee length black leather boots, crushed hat, and the Highway Patrol patch on his left shoulder. To further piss off Nordstrom, he had on a Sam Browne belt instead of a regulation gun belt, with a blue lanyard running down from his epaulet, attached to the butt of his .38 Smith and Wesson revolver. His weapon was in a flap-over holster. It was totally non-regulation stuff for patrol cops.

The Viking spoke, "Well, well, sleazy rider, looks like Mayor Beame took away your little bike for a while. Put the wire back in your hat, ditch the jackboots and those fucking homo pants, and show up tomorrow looking like a street cop. And while you're at it, detach that motherfucking cord from your gun! What the fuck— are you afraid you're gonna lose it?"

After reaming out Dennihy, he latched onto seventeen year veteran, Chester Podolsky, a helicopter pilot from the Aviation Unit. He had on the crushed hat, and wore the Aviation Unit patch. "Hey, flyboy, it looks like you're going to be grounded for a long time. Tell you what, *Sky King,* tomorrow morning, you and everyone else from your bullshit, tit details will look like real street cops at my roll call."

Podolsky was politically connected on the job through the Pulaski Association, a small, but very powerful fraternal organization of Polish and Slavic cops. He was not a man to be messed with. Chester was the sacrificial lamb from his unit. They told him that he'd be back in less than a month. This was sort of *the check's in the mail* handjob. Sven Nordstrom had made some more enemies, and it would soon be his undoing. He was not screwing with rookies here, but guys who had been around the block a few times, and were not intimidated by anyone, on or off the job.

Standing next to Podolsky was a man who would eventually become his partner, P.O. Henry Mulligan. He was a pilot with the Harbor Precinct and commanded a police launch throughout the navigable waters of New York City. Mulligan had a very prestigious position, but like his partner, they were being sent back to the trenches. Mulligan was a sixteen year veteran, as well as a Chief in the United States Naval Reserve. Nordstrom, seeing the Harbor Precinct shoulder patch with the anchor, said "Your little boat just sank, Admiral. You're a street cop now. Dress like one."

That fateful day would bring forth more colorful characters to the 13th Precinct. P.O. Vincent Quaranta was one of them. He worked undercover in the Manhattan South Public Morals Division, infiltrating unlicensed gay bars and clubs. Because of his short stature and swarthy Sicilian complexion, Vinny's nickname on the job was "Sabu." Sgt. Nordstrom knew Quaranta somewhat, and because Vinny had developed some effeminate mannerisms from his undercover work, he asked him in front of the platoon if he was "half a fag." The veteran cops all got the message that the Viking was an A-1, rat-bastard scumbag.

After arraigning my tree top burglars, I came back to the Precinct around noon, and reported back to the desk officer, Lieutenant Carl Cantorwicz. The Lieutenant was a heavy set, bald, jovial man, in his late-fifties, who was so well-liked in the Precinct that the men rarely addressed him as "Lieutenant", or even "Loo." They meant no disrespect, and simply called him "Uncle Carl," since he reminded every cop of their favorite uncle. He was a World War II veteran who chain smoked cigars while on the desk. Carl had a quick wit and could have been a Catskill comedian, had he wanted to be.

Lt. Cantorwicz knew that I made a good arrest, and my partner had been laid off, so he threw me a bone and told me to stay in the station house for the rest of the tour and relieve the switchboard operator. I was glad to do so, until Uncle Carl went to lunch, and was replaced by Sgt. Nordstrom, The Viking.

About 12:30 P.M. a stunningly beautiful woman came into the Precinct. Her name was Daphne Young from the Wentworth Advertising Company on Park Avenue South. She was tall and slim, with long, reddish-brown hair, and her lavender dress was cut low in front, showing a lot of cleavage, and two beautiful breasts. Top that off with a sexy British accent, and you had one very attractive woman. She told Sergeant Nordstrom that she was trying to find a macho looking male model to work in a proposed commercial for a linen company which made wrinkle-free sheets. Basically, the photo would show a scared female Marine Corps recruit being browbeaten by a U.S.M.C. Drill Sergeant, because there were wrinkles in her bed sheets. The caption under the photo was to read "If she only used our brand of sheets, this would not have happened."

The Viking, supreme egotist that he was, quickly nominated himself to be the Drill Sergeant. Ms. Young gave Nordstrom her card and said that she would call him in a week or two. As she left, I noticed that she looked great from behind, too. Sven stood there, preening, beaming and dreaming of his entry into show business. My mental wheels started spinning about how to turn this thing around to fuck Nordstrom right up his *squarehead* ass, as revenge for humiliating veteran cops in front of everyone.

Adding further to our misery, our union delegate advised us the next day that our pay was being cut by more than sixty dollars per week, because the city was broke.

MY NEW PARTNER

With Ben Harrigan gone, I was a lost soul. Until things got sorted out, I worked every day with a new partner. Aloysious Jackson was a black cop who worked in Harlem. Jackson was two weeks away form being promoted to detective, when a spiteful supervisor put him on the list to go back to patrol. He could have been a bitter man, but he always came to work with a positive demeanor, and was a pleasure to work with. Al had worked in the 6th Homicide Division in Harlem for two years, making dozens of murder arrests, and had a 100% conviction rate. Al Jackson was one great cop.

I also worked with a man named Fred Davidovich, who was a licensed electrician. He used to do all of the electrical repairs for the NYPD. Fred could fix anything electronic, and thus, his nickname in the Precinct became "Mr. Wizard."

Another good guy was P.O. Wayne Harrision, from the Warrant Squad. Wayne's wife had become a drug addict, and she repeatedly sent letters to the Police Commissioner, accusing him of some outrageous act. When the list of transfers came out, Wayne's name was put on the top, just to get rid of the former Mrs. Harrison.

After the first week, a new cop came into the 13th Precinct. His name was Tommy McInerney, a funny, wise cracking cop from Queens. Tommy worked in the Property Clerk Division and got the axe late, having pissed off his Commanding Officer.

When evidence is no longer needed, the Property Clerk throws things like tools and knives in the garbage. Of course, if an item is in good condition, it winds up on the basement work bench of one of the cops who works there. 'No harm, no foul' was the prevailing thought. The C.O., Deputy Inspector Arthur Miles, was trying to stop this from happening, and asked for Tommy's input. McInerney responded "What's the problem, boss.......... how many fucking screwdrivers can one guy use?"

It was not the answer that the Inspector was looking for, and the humorless, dry balls Miles sent Tommy packing to the 13th Precinct.

Tommy McInerney's locker was a couple of spaces from mine. We hit it off well. We had both been NYPD Trainees for three years prior to becoming Police Officers. We were promoted to Police Officer on our 21st birthdays and Tommy was two years younger than me.

When I first met McInerney, I thought of my younger brother, Frank, who was stricken with schizophrenia at age nineteen. Frank was a good brother, fine athlete, and friend, who had become a veritable vegetable overnight. The loss of my brother to this dreaded, little understood disease, ripped my heart out. I was happy to team up with this younger officer, since it made up a bit for my great personal loss. I could never understand why God had cursed my family for doing this to our Frank, virtually taking his life away, without actually killing him, and irreparably harming us forever.

Going to work was fun again. The Long Island clique was being broken up slowly, but there was still some hard core left. Being with Tommy for eight hours a day was a breeze. The new *layoff cops* may have been a disgruntled bunch, but they were dependable, hard-working police officers.

I relayed the story to my new partner about Sgt. Nordstrom ridiculing the veterans at roll call, and also about Ms. Daphne Young from the advertising agency. Tommy said "Jimmy, it's time to pay The Viking back. His big ego will be his undoing. Do you know any girls who can do voices for different ethnic groups?"

I immediately thought of Margie Fogarty, from the Visual Aids Unit of the Police Academy, where they did the training films. She used to do the voice-overs. Margie was a regular at the Anawanda

Club, and was a barrel of laughs, especially when she got her load on. Also, she could be trusted to keep her mouth shut. This woman could do the voices of just about any ethnic group.

OPERATION SWORDSMAN

Margie signed on for *Operation Swordsman* and was sworn to secrecy. (In police jargon, *swordsman* means a womanizer). We picked a day when Sgt. Nordstrom was working as the desk officer. Nordstrom answered the desk phone and a woman's voice with a British accent asked for Sergeant Sven Nordstrom.

"Yes, this is Sergeant Nordstrom."

"Sergeant, this is Daphne Young, from Wentworth Advertising. We met about two weeks ago."

The Viking was beside himself and said "Yes, Ms. Young, of course I remember you. What can I do for you?"

"Well, Sergeant, I have looked all over the New York City for my model for the sheet commercial. But, of all the men I interviewed, *you* were the most macho. I want *you* for the role of the United States Marine Corps Drill Sergeant. Are you interested in the job?"

Nordstrom did not even have to think. "Of course, Ms. Young, when do you want me to come in?"

"We are shooting tomorrow afternoon, Sergeant, about 5:00 P.M. But one thing, you must have a Marine Corps Drill Sergeant's uniform. You can rent one from a theatrical equipment store. The company will reimburse you for the expense. And, to be realistic, you must have to have a Marine Corps haircut, so that you look the part for the photo shoot."

"O.K., Ms. Young, I'll see you tomorrow at 5:00 P M. at your Park Avenue South studio."

In her sexy voice, she purred into his ear "Ciao, Sergeant."

The big fish had taken the bait. Nordstrom found a theatrical supply shop on West 28th Street and Broadway and rented the

Drill Sergeant's outfit, complete with Smokey the Bear hat. The next day he got off work at 3:30 P.M. and immediately went to Sal the barber on Third Avenue for a skinhead haircut. Off The Viking strode to Park Avenue South for his grand entry into show biz.

At 4:55 P.M., NYPD Sgt. Sven Nordstrom, newly promoted to United States Marine Corps Gunnery Sergeant, promptly arrived at the Wentworth Advertising Company on Park Avenue South and met the receptionist. The place was decorated with real flowers and dark wood, and reeked of "old money."

Approaching the reception desk, he said "Hi, I'm Sergeant Nordstrom from the 13th Precinct, and I'm here for my appointment with Ms. Young."

The pudgy, middle aged, blonde receptionist with huge breasts, puffed deeply on her Chesterfield, and said in a husky, pre-cancerous rasp "Sgt. Nordstrom, there is a Ms. Young here, but she has no appointments today; she is out of town."

"No, ma'am, you don't understand. I'm Sergeant Nordstrom from the 13th Precinct. I'm here to do the photo shoot for the commercial as the Marine Corps Drill Sergeant."

"Well, Sergeant, there is no photo shoot today, and we have none scheduled for at least two weeks. You must be mistaken."

By this time, Nordstrom was ready to blow. His beloved blonde hair had been shorn down to the scalp like an Australian sheep, and the lovely Daphne Young was nowhere to be found.

"Could you at least call Ms. Young for me and tell her that Sgt. Nordstrom is here for the commercial?"

"I would, Sergeant, but she's in England on vacation. And besides, we don't do any filming here, anyway. This is just our office for paperwork and stuff."

Nordstrom's massive ego had been deflated. He now realized that he has not just been fucked............ he has been butt-fucked real good, with no foreplay, no lube, and no KY jelly. And he can't figure out who did it. He has screwed so many cops, and been such a nasty prick, that he can't imagine who might have done this to him. There were just too many suspects.

The walk back to the Precinct seemed a lot longer to Gunnery Sergeant Nordstrom, with passersby gawking at the out-of-place Drill Instructor. As he bolted into the station house, the first person he met was the desk officer, Lt. Otto von Richter. He took one look at Nordstrom in his USMC outfit and shaved head, and burst out laughing.

The Viking failed to see the humor in it all and screamed out "I'll get the mother-fucker who did this to me! I'll rip his head off, and shit down his fucking neck! He'll curse his own mother for ever having given fucking birth to him."

By now, the entire Precinct staff was howling with laughter, and Nordstrom was reduced to the horse's ass that he always was.

Of course, Tommy and I were in the station house at the time, and we knew enough not to let him see us laugh, or Nordstrom might have suspected us as the culprits.

Score one for the good guys. From the Book of Cynical Proverbs comes the old adage "Revenge is a dish best served cold."

THE MOON DOGS
OF THE MIDNIGHT SHIFT

The patrol cops' schedule had us working one week of midnight shifts every six weeks. It was a terrible work chart, and difficult to adjust to. There was a group of cops who worked the midnight shift on a steady basis, called the Moon Dogs. I tended to look at them with a jaundiced eye. They were, for the most part, an unmotivated group of Long Islanders, who put in the minimal effort on any given day. Worse still, I looked on them as unreliable as cops.

The summer in Manhattan can be unbearable for radio car crews. The black pavement and tar roofs soaked up the daytime heat and kept them hot throughout the night. My partner and I were both pretty fit guys, but we would lose five or more pounds a shift, only to regain it after work by drinking beer. Due to the shortage of cops, we were working harder, for less money, with older men. Typically, we were handling over twenty-five calls per tour, and it seemed like everyone who called the police lived on the fifth floor of a walk-up. Most sectors were now doubled up.

Still, the midnight shift seemed fairly dull this night. It was just the routine stuff of stabbings, drunks, vehicle accidents and family fights. The 13th was a sociologist's dream. If you wanted diversity, there was plenty of it. With one call, you were on Gramercy Park West where some rich, white WASP couple were arguing because the wife spent five grand on clothes. On the next radio run, you were in a tenement apartment on E. 26th Street, between Second and Third Avenues, where a drunken husband knocked his wife's teeth out for burning the pork chops.

The Moon Dogs were from the hard core of Long Islanders

38

and had their own car pool. They engineered it so that they always had the early split, starting at 11:30 P.M. and ending at 7:30 A.M. The non-car poolers started and ended a half hour later.

It was 7:15 A.M. and all I could think about was getting off work in less than an hour, and having three days off. Suddenly, the dispatcher's alarm button sounded and called for a 13th Precinct unit to handle a call of a man with a knife on the fifth floor of the Elton Hotel on East 26th Street. Although it was not our sector, we took off for the Elton. En route, the dispatcher advised us that the man also started a fire in his room. I kept waiting to hear what other units were responding, but the radio was silent.

"What the fuck is going on?", I said aloud. "Isn't this the NYPD? Where the hell is the back-up? Aren't any other radio cars coming?"

What cop wouldn't come to assist another cop? So much for brotherhood in this precinct, I thought.

We pulled up and parked on Park Avenue South near the hotel. The Elton was a welfare hotel, and a total shithouse. The lobby smelled like a mixture of stale piss and fresh vomit. The rodent-faced desk clerk informed us that the man in room 502 had started a fire in his room and pulled a knife on him when he went to investigate. He sounded like he was bullshitting, but I couldn't be sure.

The rickety elevator made us wish we had walked up the stairs. Turning left, we found room 502, the last one in a long hallway. The door felt hot, indicating a fire in the room. Upon knocking, the door swung completely open. There, standing in the doorway was a tall, shirtless, tattooed white man with a shaved head, weighing well over 250 pounds. He held a Bowie knife in his left hand and said "I'm gonna kill you."

I had my gun out and pointed it right at the man's chest. Tommy was right behind me in the narrow hallway. All of a sudden, my knees turned to jello, and I had never felt this scared in my life. I just knew I had to drill this psycho bastard. There is an old saying that when you are about to die you see your entire life in front of you. In my case, all I saw were flashes of my kindergarten teacher, Mrs. McDonald, making butter in the classroom of P.S. 3, circa 1951. What recessed part of my brain did that come from?

The man with the knife came closer, then he stopped abruptly, less than two feet away from me. As I pulled back on the trigger, the hammer went slowly into firing position. We were at a standoff. I never saw myself as a killer, and always tried to avoid shooting someone. However, this scenario was not of my making. To make it worse, there was a fire in the guy's bed that was starting to spread. It didn't take an Einstein or a Newton to figure out that this entire flea bag hotel would be engulfed by fire if we didn't do something soon.

Our adversary with the knife did not come any closer, so I jerked him off by telling him that we went to the wrong room. I reached out with my nightstick and used the leather thong to loop around the door knob and shut the door. Tommy had a good idea.

"I'm going to get a metal box spring to put over the doorway."

The first person to open their door was a wizened old man. Tommy brushed him aside and said "Police emergency, pop," then whipped the mattress off his bed and took the metal box spring, leaving the old geezer standing in his jockey shorts, bewildered, confused, and muttering to himself in the middle of his room.

The box spring was placed over the doorway, and not a moment too soon. We put in another call for help, and again, no 13th Pct. radio cars responded. The dispatcher frantically kept asking for 13th Precinct units to assist 13 Adam-Boy, but nobody answered. Just like the time with Mazzrella and Conner, nobody could give a damn about another cop. Just don't miss the car pool.

Without any warning, the door to room 502 opened and our man with the knife became enraged upon seeing his doorway blocked with the box spring.

We were now in a death struggle with this madman, who was pushing on the box spring with all of his strength, while we were pushing back. With his left hand, he was trying to stab us through the box spring, but he couldn't reach us. Tommy frantically called for help over the radio, but still, there was no response. We were physically exhausted trying to fight this huge man off, and we couldn't hold on much longer.

It was now almost 7:30 A.M. and inside the station house, a very pissed off Sergeant Byrne was listening to the radio at the desk and heard our frantic calls for help.

Byrne was the day shift patrol supervisor. He grabbed his driver, veteran officer Danny Delladonna, and they bolted from the Precinct, hell-bent to respond to the Elton. Danny roared out of the station house block with lights and siren.

The Sergeant's car turned north on Park Avenue South, then east on East 26th Street. It was great to finally hear the sirens as we were battling this knife-wielding lunatic. When Sgt. Byrne and P.O. Delladonna arrived on the fifth floor, the supervisor quickly sized up the situation and called for the Emergency Service Division.

In the NYPD, patrol cops say "When a citizen needs help, he calls a cop. When a cop needs help, he calls the Emergency Service Division." The ESD is an elite unit that handles everything that other cops can't. Since Emergency Service Unit One shared the same building with the 13th Pct., most of the patrol cops and ESU men knew one another, mostly from hanging out at the Anawanda Club.

Within minutes, Richie Harris and Paul Rivetski, from ESU One, arrived and knew what to do. Rivetski loaded the tear gas gun and let one go into the room. The knife man had retreated deeper into his room upon seeing the ESU men. He was not too crazy, because he opened his window to get fresh air, and washed his face in the sink.

"Fuck you!" was Rivetski's response, as his second canister hit the crazed man squarely in the chest, knocking him down. He tried to pick up the canister, but it was too hot.

The man was starting to falter a bit when Rivetski delivered

41

the *coup de grace* with the third canister. The ESU men charged in with large shields and batons and pinned him to the floor. Tommy disarmed the man of the knife. Due to the prisoner's tremendous size, we had to link our handcuffs together just to rear cuff him.

It was off to Bellevue with our prisoner, where they washed him down and removed all traces of tear gas from him. He was kept in the hospital for observation, and charged with arson, menacing, possession of a weapon, and resisting arrest.

When I came back to the Precinct from court, I was confronted by some empty suit Deputy Inspector from headquarters. He started to grill me on why so much force was used just to arrest one man. I wanted to choke the fool. I could have legally shot the guy, and probably have gotten a medal, but I did everything to avoid it. Now the brass in Police Plaza have a problem with it?

The D.I. worked for a Deputy Chief in headquarters, Roland Martinson. The Chief was an obese, billowing, bulbous buffoon, who fancied himself as the reincarnation of General George S. Patton. Physically and mentally, however, he more resembled Field Marshal Hermann Göering. He heard the incident on his radio while driving to work, and decided that the tactics were not proper. I was so pissed off I said to the Inspector "You shouda been there, boss."

After that interlude, Sergeant Byrne took me aside and said "Jimmy, what those guys on the late shift did to you and McInerney was wrong. This is not the end of it. I am personally going to see to it that they get their shit together."

That night, I came to work about 11:20 P.M. and proceeded to the locker room. The first person I saw was the ringleader of the Moondogs, Jeremiah P. Logan. He was a do-nothing cop who had accomplished nothing in his fifteen years on the job. Logan and his boys were having coffee that morning when Tommy and I responded to the call at the Elton. They heard our calls for help, but did not want to interfere with their car pool. They were an unremorseful bunch. Upon approaching Logan, I asked why he and his partner did not respond to our call for help.

His answer was "Listen, kid, I live in Long Island, and I need my car pool to get home. If you are so fucking stupid to answer the radio at 7:15 in the morning, you deserve everything that happens to you."

By now, I could have had a stroke I was so angry. Getting in Logan's face, I said "Listen up, numb nuts, I have eleven years on the job, and some big tub of shit like you does not call me *kid*. If you ever punk out on a call for help from another cop, I'll personally put you in the hospital, and you *will* miss your car pool – for a couple of fucking weeks."

After I made my point, Sgt. Byrne grabbed the Moondogs and told them that he would not tolerate any more cowardice or lethargy from his clique. The term *cowardice* stung Logan and his boys, who had such a low sense of duty that they did not even realize they were doing anything wrong. After the meeting with Sgt. Byrne, the message got through, very clearly.

It was not worth telling the midnight shift Sergeant, "Wild Bill" Hanley. Wild Bill had just gotten off of a 30 day suspension for being drunk on duty. Not just drunk, but he actually thought that he was making a daring rescue of someone trapped in a second floor tenement fire. The "victim" simply walked down the stairs to the street. However, there was Hanley, swinging on the fire escape, like some emaciated, toothless Tarzan, trying to save the man. Hanley had to be rescued by two NYFD Firefighters with a ladder. A Battalion Chief saw the incident and reported it. Then off went Hanley to "the farm" to dry out. Hanley was no stranger to the farm, having been a guest three times before, courtesy of Monsignor Francis Dunphy, the Catholic Chaplain.

"WE'RE PROFESSIONAL POLICE OFFICERS"

Our sector, 13 Adam-Boy, went from the East River to 2nd Avenue, and 14th Street to 30th Street. A good part of the sector was Stuyvesant Town and Peter Cooper Village. Right after World War II, the Metropolitan Life Insurance Company purchased large tracts of land along the East River, between East 14th and East 23rd Streets, then a shanty town of mostly Irish immigrants. Met Life razed the wooden shacks and built an impressive apartment complex, with modest rents for working class and middle class people. They had their own security force, and there was rarely a call there. That's why the radio run to apartment 6G at 13 Stuyvesant Oval seemed out of place.

The call was to investigate threats to a woman. We were buzzed into the lobby and proceeded to the 6th floor, where we were met by a middle aged woman with the most miserable, sour looking face I ever saw in my life. She looked like she had been eating nothing but lemons for months.

The complainant, Alison Lockman, was a teacher at the nearby public school on E. 20th Street. She explained that a former student, Felix Camacho, had been taunting her for weeks, by calling her names in public.

Tommy asked her "Well, Ms. Lockman, what names is Felix calling you?"

"If I tell you, you'll laugh," the teacher said.

I said "Ms. Lockman, we're professional police officers, you can tell us. We won't laugh."

"Are you sure you won't laugh?"

44

"Of course, ma'am, so what was Felix calling you?"

"Well.......he called me......*Pickle Puss.*"

I couldn't help looking over at Tommy and we were both busting our guts trying not to laugh. As I was making out the report, I got to the words "Pickle Puss" and completely lost it after looking at the woman's sour mug once more. Once I started laughing, McInerney started, and we could not stop.

The outraged woman began screaming "You said you wouldn't laugh. Get the hell out of my home, you two bastards! Get the hell out, right now! Some *professional police officers* you are! I'm going to report you."

We bolted out of the apartment, laughing like two loons, with Pickle Puss flailing her pocketbook, hitting Tommy in the back several times. Once we got back into the radio car, it took us a few minutes before we could stop laughing.

Sure enough, Alison Lockman's letter arrived at the Precinct and she came in to see Captain Fitzgerald. From his room, the Captain could see her standing in front of the desk. He took one look at her face and locked himself in his bathroom, hysterical with laughter. This World War II veteran of hand-to-hand combat in the Pacific, with four amphibious landings at Guadalcanal, Iwo Jima, Tarawa and Okinawa, could not control himself. About five minutes later he got out of the bathroom and assured the complainant that McInerney and Kavanaugh would be sent for sensitivity training, presumably, along with himself.

"SO, WHO KNEW?"

Sometimes on the midnight shift it gets slow, even in the summer. Due to a shortage of manpower, Tommy and I now had sectors Adam, Boy, Charlie and David on the 12 X 8 shift. Our patrol area went from 14th to 30th Streets, and Fifth Avenue to the East River. Population wise, it was larger than many American cities.

The Public Morals Division crackdown on prostitution in Times Square brought scores of hookers south to the East 20's. "Johns" drove around looking to pick up the girls, and it was a game of cat and mouse, between the cops, the Johns and the hookers. Prostitution was a low level crime, and police managers did not want to waste a lot of manpower on it. The idea was to keep them moving and harass the customers.

East 24th Street and Third Avenue was still a nice, respectable area, and half a dozen or so hookers standing near the front door of the Gloccamorra stood out. The "Glocc" was a real donkey joint, with Irish music every night. It was a big cop and fireman hangout, and the manager, Barney McHugh, did not want the girls hustling out in front of his place. Most of his customers were so loaded they couldn't have gotten it up in a windstorm, anyway.

I got out of the radio car and grabbed one hooker whom I had told three times to get out of the area. She had a major attitude, with that *Leave me alone; I'm just making an honest living* look on her face. She was a nice looking black kid, probably about 19, but like most prostitutes, she looked a lot older than her actual age. Over all, she was about an eight, but she had a number ten ass. Her black skirt was slit up to her pubic hairs. Fed up with her crap, I took her pocketbook and dumped the contents out on the sidewalk. There were about a dozen condoms there, and I took them all.

Opening my shirt, I took out the large pin that held my shield in place, and punctured holes in all of the Trojans. The broad freaked out and said "*What the fuck do you think you're doing, cop?*"

Without missing a beat I said "I'm only doing what you were going to do with them, honey. I'm putting a little prick in them."

That put her out of commission for the night.

Usually the Madison Avenue area is dead at night. The major businesses of Met Life and New York Life were closed up. It was normally a daytime district. The Appellate Division of the New York State Supreme Court was on East 25th Street, just off of Madison Avenue. It was an impressive looking building, with a parking lot adjacent to it.

At 2 A.M. nothing was going down, so we decided to take a break and have a coffee in the lot next to the Appellate Division. As we pulled up, there was a beat up brown and white Ford station wagon in the extreme end of the parking lot, lights out, with the back of the car facing the rear wall. I could make out the hazy figure of a man in the front seat, but nothing else. We drove by and pretended that we didn't notice the car.

After going around the block, we parked out on the street, and walked up to the station wagon on foot. There, in the front seat was a Hasidic Jew, jerkin' his gherkin for all he was worth. In the back seat was another Hasidic man with his pants around his ankles, getting a blow job from a black hooker. Both men were in full Hasidic uniform: black beaver hat, black pants, white shirt, and black jacket; and they both reeked with body odor that would have made a vulture gag.

"What the fuck?" I thought, "Aren't these guys supposed to be religious?"

And what about the hooker? She must be getting combat pay to blow these two foul smelling *cheese dicks.*"

The Hasidim and the hooker were oblivious to us watching them. Tommy, in a bit of sadism, waited until the guy in the back, whom he called "Heshie," was just about to hit the paradise stroke. We shined our flashlights on the occupants, and they panicked. The hooker, having been caught *in flagrante delicto*, could say nothing. Of course, it's not polite to speak with your mouth full.

"Everyone, get out of this car!" we commanded.

Out came "Heshie" from the back seat, and "Schlomo" from the front seat. The tall, slim, hooker looked on sheepishly, as only one was caught completely wrong could look.

I started giving them the morality lecture, while Tommy looked on amused as hell. The men were cunning and playing stupid, saying things like "Vhut ees blow jub? I dun't know that vurd."

I was losing my patience with the men and said to them "You're getting blow jobs from some *schwartze* whore, and it isn't even a woman."

Simultaneously, Tommy whipped the wig off of the hooker, only to reveal a six foot tall buck named Dexter Carter, from Bedford Stuyvesant.

Heshie exclaimed out loud " So, who knew?"

We put nothing on paper. All of them were told to get lost, and we laughed all night long.

PAYDAY

Payday in the NYPD was every other Thursday. Since the City of New York went broke, it became more and more difficult for us to cash our paychecks. Banks would hassle us and find one lame excuse after another for not cashing our checks, fearing that they would bounce. It was not a problem for Mr. McSorley, the proprietor of the Anawanda Club on E. 20th Street and 2nd Avenue.

Old man McSorley and his son, Tim, knew that cops liked to drink after work. He was heavily into Democratic Party politics and was assured that no cop's checks would ever bounce. Thereupon, McSorley sought out the Patrolmen's Benevolent Association delegate from the 13th Pct., "Loud Lenny" Lantini. The deal was made that on payday afternoons, a police department radio car would escort Mr. McSorley and his son to the bank on East 14th Street and 2nd Avenue. McSorley would withdraw enough money to cash every cop customer's check, and then be driven back to the Anawanda Club with the money.

It was the classic *quid pro quo:* Every cop's paycheck would be cashed, and McSorley was guaranteed a full house every other Thursday. This routine went on for weeks, and a cast of characters soon blossomed from it. One flashy eccentric was Victor Velez, a handsome, divorced man from the Bronx. He came to work every day with a sport jacket, pressed trousers, and crisply ironed shirt. He got bounced from Bronx Narcotics over a bogus civilian complaint from a drug dealer. It was initially unfounded, but the dealer complained to his local Councilman, who pursued the issue. It was a totally baseless complaint, but Victor's ballless boss caved into political pressure and sent him back to patrol. His one peccadillo was that on payday, he became a binge drinker.

As soon as Victor came in and cashed his paycheck the bartender poured several Bacardi and Cokes for him. They were downed in about twenty minutes, and that was the beginning of the evening for Victor. One strange thing about Velez, however, was that after his sixth drink, he stripped down to his shorts, and stayed like that for the rest of the night on the bar stool. Nobody knew why. After a while, nobody even noticed him.

The 13th Pct. was called "Bedpan Alley" because there were so many hospitals in the neighborhood. The Anawanda had nurses from Cabrini, Bellevue, Beth Israel, Joint Diseases, and the V.A. Hospital at any given time. Cops and nurses are naturally attracted to each other. They both see the real world every day through the same jaded eyes, share the same sense of humor, and shun those who don't, or won't, see the world as they do.

Like cops, nurses see the lousy side of life, day in and day out, and receive little or no recognition from those they are helping. At least the nurses could cash their paychecks in a bank, and not a bar.

One more character who drank at the Anawanda Club was a delightful man named "Freddie", a man in his late seventies who walked with a slight limp and played the spoons for drinks. Actually, the guy was pretty good. Manhattan certainly had its strange characters.

THE DEMISE
OF THE PLUMED CAVALIER

Vinny "Sabu" Quaranta, late of Manhattan South Public Morals, was teamed up with Terry Molloy, a handsome Irishman from Brooklyn's Gerritsen Beach section. Terry had a 1950's pompadour haircut, hence his new nickname of "Teen Angel." Molloy was married to a hot tempered Brooklyn girl, a *Bensonhurst Bombshell,* the former Angelina Langellotti. She had a body that most men would leave their wife and kids for. One of the problems in their marriage was Angelina's brother, who was a major car thief in Brooklyn. It pissed off Terry greatly to see his brother-in-law, Carmine Langellotti, driving around in stolen Caddys and Lincolns all the time.

Just over a month before, Terry was on patrol in plainclothes and saw Carmine whizzing by in a stolen Cadillac. He pulled him over and slapped him around a bit. Angelina was extremely protective of her brother, and did not speak to Terry for weeks.

Then, to show what an absolute loser he was, Carmine made a civilian complaint against Terry, but failed to report that he was driving a stolen car at the time. The complaint got canned, but when the roster for guys going back to patrol was filled out for the Youth Division, Terry made the list.

Molloy had a drinking problem, but managed it well in his controlled environment, i.e., his non-drinking Italian wife constantly nagging him about his boozing. After coming to the 13th Precinct, temperance was a virtue from the past for this boy. He soon managed to be a regular at the Anawanda Club, even though Angelina did not want him drinking. They had been to

51

counseling over and over, without success.

Of course, to be a ball-buster to his Irish brother-in-law, Carmine gave Angelina a birthday gift of a 6 foot tall ceramic statue of a plumed cavalier; with the feathers, add another foot and a half. It was one of the most *guinea gaudy* things ever created. Terry hated the statue, and would remove it from the living room, and put it in the bedroom. Angelina would reverse the process, and so it went for over a year.

One night Terry got so ripped at the Anawanda, that he could not drive home, so I dropped him off at his house in Gerritsen Beach on my way home to Staten Island. Upon entering his second floor apartment on Beacon Place, the first thing he saw was the despised cavalier standing guard in the living room. This was the equivalent of waving a red flag in the face of a drunken bull.

In an alcohol fueled, hate filled rage, Terry picked up the sixty pound cavalier and screamed out "Fuck this guinea statue, and fuck your thieving, greaseball brother, too", as he threw the cavalier through the picture window. It landed below in dozens of pieces.

Angelina came out of the bedroom screaming "Get the fuck out of here, you drunken bum! Stay the fuck out, and don't come back!"

Terry never saw her again, but he sure as hell saw her lawyer a few times. Then, there was also the grand he had to pay the landlord for the picture window.

The poor plumed cavalier went the way of Humpty Dumpty, and could never be put back together again; and neither could Terry's marriage.

BAPTISM OF FIRE

The first three weeks on patrol after the Elton Hotel incident were great. The Long Island clique was broken up slowly, and the new guys started to gel. The camaraderie was there, and morale was high, even among men whose careers had been derailed, delayed, and even destroyed. There was a feeling of "What the hell can they do to us now? We're already on patrol."

Max's Kansas City Restaurant on E. 17th Street and Park Avenue South was a popular hangout for locals and tourists. It was right across the street from Union Square Park. Max' was a nice, well-run place, and never had any problems with fights or drunks.

The Devils on Wheels motorcycle gang had a headquarters thirteen blocks south, on East 4th Street. They were always getting into fights with their neighbors and baiting cops. It was July 21st, and one very hot, humid day. Tommy and I were working the 4 x 12 shift, and by 7:00 P.M. the radio was eerily quiet for a summer night in the big city.

At 7:05 P.M., twenty members of the Devils came into Max's and began to beat the owner, employees and customers, because they were annoyed over a perceived insult a week before. The phone was ripped off the wall to prevent calls to the police. An alert cook picked up a phone in the back and called 911 and reported the brawl.

A moment later, the dispatcher's alert button sounded as he reported a large fight in the 13th Precinct, at Max's Kansas City Restaurant. The first unit to respond was sector Eddie-Frank, who was a block away. The radio car team was Manny Lopez and Aloysius Jackson.

Lopez was a tenth degree dan black belt in karate, and until a few weeks ago, was an instructor in the Police Academy gym. His fists were like rocks, and capable of breaking bricks and two by fours in one blow. Jackson, who was built like a linebacker, came from the 6th Homicide Division in Harlem. He was a good man to have in a fight.

Tommy quickly responded to report Adam-Boy as also responding, but we were all the way by the East River. A month before we may have been the only unit responding, and would have taken a good beating. Next, I heard that Mazzarella and Conner in sector Charlie-David were also going.

Then, unexpectedly, Sgt. Jerry Hoffman, leader of the 13th Precinct Conditions squad, announced that he too was coming. Hoffman was a mountain of a man, about 6'5" and 260 lbs., with flaming red hair. His Conditions Squad was sent all over the Precinct to correct certain problems that the Commanding Officer wanted addressed, but would rather not want to know how they were handled. The junkies, methadonians and lowlifes of the 13th Precinct all feared Sgt. Hoffman and his men, like the vampire feared the cross and garlic cloves.

Sector Eddie-Frank was the first to respond, only to be met with the horrible scene of the motorcycle gang beating the beejeesus out of everyone in sight. The leader of the Devils was a hulking figure, with a giant beer belly, long greasy blonde hair and shaggy beard. He quickly sized up the 5'9" Lopez and his partner, and roared out "Look, someone called the cops and all they could send was a little spic and a spook."

Manny was infuriated. He stared down the ringleader, and with one swift karate move, he hit him with all of his might with a shot in the solar plexus. Mr. Mouth went down like a large oak tree falling and he would not be getting up any time soon.

Jackson had already dispatched two combatants with a right cross and a nightstick to the shins and head. Three down, and seventeen to go. Lopez and Jackson heard the sirens and knew that help was on the way. Just as we came in, one goon jumped on Al Jackson's back and tried to choke him. I pried him off by putting my nightstick under his chin and choking the stupid bastard until he couldn't breathe. Jackson then knocked him out cold.

Manny was in full combat mode, and his black belt training paid off. All who challenged him were laid out on the floor.

Now it was four against a dozen. Like a bull in a china shop, in barged Sgt. Hoffman, and his driver, Police Officer Pete Lanza, a barrel chested Vietnam veteran, and former Bronx street brawler. Neither man was endowed with the social graces, but both were reliable as hell when things got physical. Those motorcycle gang members left standing saw Sgt. Hoffman come in with his nightstick swinging, and they knew it was all over for them. They made a valiant effort to fight back, but were severely beaten, but not before one jerk hit Hoffman off the head with a beer bottle. It had no effect, other than to piss him off. The Sergeant then took his heavy cocabola stick and opened up the man's head with it. As he gave him the *wood shampoo,* Hoffman said "Shame on your ass, muthafucka'."

Pete Lanza confronted a big man and broke his jaw with one shot. It was good guys against bad guys, and the good guys won this one. In ten long minutes, order was restored to Max's. More importantly, the new group of former strangers had engaged in battle together, and emerged victorious. It was like a squad of infantry soldiers who had survived their first firefight. Incredibly, the elitist clientele of Max's was so grateful for having been rescued from these goons, that there was not even one civilian complaint claiming police brutality.

Tommy and I both realized that the climate in the 13th Precinct was changing for the better. This group of cops was becoming the NYPD that I knew and loved.

"YOU'RE ONLY A COP"

At 5 P.M. Lt. Cantorwicz called us into the station house. As he puffed on his Cohiba cigar Uncle Carl said "Boys, this is coming from the C.O., so don't blame me. There's this young broad from the local paper, the Gramercy Herald, who got permission from the Deputy Commissioner of Public Information to ride in a radio car. The old man nominated you two guys for the job. She seems like a snotty, feminist bitch, with a piss-poor attitude, if you ask me. Keep her at arms length."

Upon meeting Amy Schultz, it was mutual, instant dislike. She was a cop-hating, super liberal type, who was never exposed to the real world. She had an extreme left wing agenda and was hell bent to report that way, regardless of the facts. You can't win with these close-minded, journalism major types, no matter what you do.

As soon as we got into the radio car, a call came over the air to investigate a family dispute at 462 2nd Avenue. As we entered apartment 9-J we were met by a black couple in their early forties. The apartment was working class, neat and orderly, and the two well-dressed children looked on very respectfully. They showed no signs of abuse or neglect.

The wife told me that her husband had slapped her during an argument, but she did not elaborate as to the cause of the dispute. After talking to the husband, it was learned that the wife went to Off Track Betting every day and blew the family finances on horse races and liquor. The husband, a truck driver, finally blew up and they got into a heated argument.

Once they calmed down, the wife declined to press charges for harassment, and that ended the matter. Of course, Amy thought differently, in that the female was always the mistreated, innocent victim in every relationship. She asked "Why did you just take the husband's word that he worked as truck driver, and the wife was a gambler and a drinker, without any further investigation?"

Looking at Tommy, I suspected that he wanted to backhand the sniveling little shrew just to shut her up. So, I said to her "What did we take at face value, and not investigate?"

In a sarcastic tone, she replied "Well, the husband said that he worked as a truck driver, and you didn't even check any further to see if he was telling the truth. Also, you never bothered to investigate the gambling or drinking allegations"

"Well, Ms. Schultz, it was very easy to see that the man was working as a truck driver, and not on welfare, and the wife was a gambler and a drinker."

Incredulously, she asked "I find it hard to believe that you could determine all of that, without even asking one question?"

I said "It was very easy. One merely has to use the powers of observation. It's the end of July and the apartment was hot. If they had been on welfare, the air conditioner would have been on full blast, because they don't have to pay for it. The working man has to pay his own bills, hence the air conditioner is used sparingly. The welfare parasite lives in the fantasy world of social services, where you can avoid all responsibility for your actions, and some taxpaying schmuck has to pick up the tab. Also, the stack of losing O.T.B. tickets on the kitchen counter was a great tip-off, as well as the Teamsters' Union magazine on the coffee table. Did you notice the half-empty bottle of Cutty Sark on top of the refrigerator? Well, working class men usually don't drink scotch, they drink beer. And if they do drink whiskey, it's rye, with a beer chaser."

My Sherlock Holmes-like logic annoyed Schultz greatly, who saw every woman and minority as a victim of society and the oppressive white majority. She was seething in the back seat of the radio car, because two supposedly lesser educated men had upstaged her with a showing of common sense. How dare the unwashed not give deference to her vastly superior Vassar and Columbia education!

Central interrupted with a call to 475 First Avenue, Apartment 16G, to investigate a suspicious smell. We were at the upscale thirty story apartment building in no time. After telling the doorman where we were going, he said nothing, only giving us a solemn nod of his head, as if he knew something very bad had happened up there, but was keeping it to himself.

As soon as we got off the elevator at the sixteenth floor, we were met by a whining, nasal, Brooklyn born, married-to-a-doctor, Jewish American Princess, named Fern Levy.

Tommy was first off the elevator and said "Did you call us ma'am?"

"Yes" replied Mrs. Levy, "I live in apartment 16F, and I haven't seen my neighbor for a few days. There is a strange smell coming out of her apartment and I suspect that something is wrong in there. She doesn't answer the door."

The smell of decayed human flesh permeated the air. If you've smelled a ripe cadaver once, you will never forget it for the rest of your life.

Tommy, long on knowledge, but short on tact, said to Mrs. Levy "It's very obvious to me that your neighbor has been dead for quite a while."

Levy was agitated. "How could you know that? You don't even have a medical degree, yet you can diagnose through a closed door? *You're only a cop.*"

How often had we heard those hurtful words from ignorant people? "*You're only a cop.*" And most of the time, it was from those we were trying to help.

Of course, Amy Schultz got into her feminist snit and said "Why can't you just listen to a woman for once?"

Ignoring her taunts, I went out onto the fire escape from Mrs. Levy's apartment and quickly made my way to the window of apartment 16G. The windows were filthy with city grime, and hadn't been washed for years. However, after brushing away some dirt, I noticed a body lying face up on the living room floor. The person had what appeared to be white hair, and a white shirt. I jimmied the window open with my knife and opened it wide enough to climb in. The sickening, disgusting odor escaping the apartment was so overwhelming that it hit me like a punch in the stomach. I reflexively blew my lunch all over the brown leather couch, then recovered, and went over to check on the woman lying on the living room floor.

I had to climb through my own puke, which didn't smell too bad, compared to the corpse. The woman had been dead about ten days. It was not white hair or a white shirt that I saw, but hundreds of teeming maggots feeding on her head and torso. Due to the intense summer heat, the body blew up and burst, sending a sickening, vile smelling liquid all over the parquet floor. Flies laid their eggs on the decayed flesh, and the hatched eggs became flesh eating maggots. The body's bloated face gave off an eerie, macabre look, and the woman's bulging eyes seemed to follow me all over the apartment.

Sergeant Jane Parker arrived, along with her driver, Neil "Numb Nuts" Noonan. At age 61, Noonan was the oldest cop in the Precinct, with 39 years on the job. He had some form of dementia, perhaps Alzheimer's Disease, but refused to retire. No boss wanted to be the bad guy and force Neil off the job, so Captain Fitzgerald made him work inside as cell attendant, and station house cleaner, who cops affectionately called "the broom." When working inside, Noonan had to give his gun to the desk officer as soon as he came into the Precinct. The only time he was allowed on the street was as Sergeant's chauffeur.

Neil left the NYPD in 1942 to serve in the United States Army for three years. He was wounded in Tunisia, in the battle of the Kasserine Pass, returned to full duty, and saw more combat in Italy and Germany before being discharged in late 1945, coming right back to the 13th Precinct.

Sgt. Parker entered the apartment and nearly vomited. She was a good boss and a hardened street cop, but this one was just too much for her. I sensed her queasiness, and motioned to the couch, saying, "It's O.K, Sarge, I called *Ralph* the minute I got in here."

Remarkably, she held it down. This lady was one tough cop.

Outside, Mrs. Doctor and Amy the reporter, were whipping themselves into a collective feminist bitch-fit over the fact that they were not allowed in to see the corpse. Sgt. Parker told them that the sight inside the apartment was something that civilians are not used to, and they would be offended at the condition of the body.

"So, it's just because we're women?" was the reporter's sarcastic jibe.

Sgt. Parker, already fed up with their crap, said "O.K, no harm in you coming in, one at a time, I guess."

Pearl Levy, whose husband is a doctor, you know, was the first one in. She saw her neighbor's naked body, which had a blackish-green hue. The body was so bloated with gases that it had burst in several places, exposing the interior of the body, as well as the face and legs. The smell was overwhelming and she said "What's that white stuff on her head and chest?"

The Sergeant told her "It's hundreds of maggots. They finished eating her hair, and now they are boring into her skull and chest cavity to feed."

With that, Mrs. Doctor gagged, did an about-face, and puked into her cupped hands. She was out the door so fast that her back draft caused the door to close. This left our college genius, the cub reporter from of the Gramercy Herald.

Amy Schultz came in, along with her nasty attitude. As soon as she saw the decomposed corpse, she proceeded to come in for a closer look. The putrid liquid oozing from the body laid down a sickening, unctuous coating on the bare wood floor. As Amy came near the body, she began to slip in the goo, and started to fall in slow motion. For three or four seconds she flailed her arms, like a baby bird trying to fly, then landed face down on top of the corpse.

Amy's weight forced foul air and maggots from the cadaver's mouth right onto her face and into her mouth.

Panicked, she got up, covered head to toe with D.O.A. slime, maggots, and large chunks of black and green decayed flesh. First, Amy spit out half a dozen maggots, then she projectile-vomited across the room. After a brief scream of horror, she bolted down the stairs and was never seen or heard from again.

"Good riddance", I thought to myself.

Tommy and I found some coffee grounds and put them in a frying pan. Burning coffee grounds is a great home remedy to counter the smell of decayed human flesh.

Coming back to the station house, we reported back to Uncle Carl, reciting all of the evening's events. The seasoned old Lieutenant leaned back in his chair and summed it all up with one puff of his cigar, as he quoted The Book of Cynical Proverbs: "Well, boys, some days you're the bug.......... and some days you're the fucking windshield."

YOU BETTER GET A LAWYER

We had just finished a day shift after handling an unusual numbers of calls. Tommy and I were beat and needed to cool down with an ice cold Bud at the Anawanda before heading home. Before I could get the second gulp of beer down, Sergeant Byrne came in and said "Tommy, Jimmy, I have to see you guys in the back room right away."

There was nobody in the dining room at 4:15 P.M., so we were there all by ourselves. Sgt. Byrne said "You remember that nut from the Elton Hotel who pulled the knife on you, and started the fire in his room? Well, I just found out that the guy died in Bellevue Hospital from pneumonia and swelling of the brain."

Tommy replied "So, what's the fuckin' problem, Sarge?"

"The problem is, boys, that every death of a person in police custody is investigated by the New York State Department of Corrections. An investigator came in the other day asking questions about how the guy was arrested. I gave him all of the facts as I knew them, and thought that it was the end of it. Turns out, that there is a new Assistant Medical Examiner who is claiming that the cause of death is a "criminal homicide." His theory is that the three tear gas canisters were unnecessary and wound up killing the man. This little bastard is whispering into the state investigator's ear, as well as the D.A.'s, and he's causing problems for all of us."

Now, I was super pissed off. "Sarge, you know damn well that we didn't kill this fucking guy. I could have lawfully shot the jerk when he pulled the knife on me, but I didn't. What the hell is going on here?"

"Jimmy, I know people inside the M.E.'s Office and they tell me that this young Ivy League asshole, Assistant M.E., is trying to make a name for himself by burning cops, and making headlines to promote himself. His attitude is 'The hell with the truth, as long as I can hang some cops to advance my career'. I went to my union delegate and he recommended a lawyer to me. You better get a lawyer, too."

"What the fuck, Sarge! I respond to a radio run of some nut with a knife who set his room on fire in a shithouse hotel. He pulls a Bowie knife on me and my partner, and I don't shoot him. Now, I have to get a fucking lawyer? Just tell me what the fuck is going on here; just what the mother-fuck is going on here?"

"Take it easy, Jimmy. My Sergeants Benevolent Association lawyer is retired NYPD Sergeant, Melvin Weinberg. This guy has balls like a wild bull elephant. He loves to investigate and research, and he knows his stuff. But, you better call the Patrolmens' Benevolent Association and get your own lawyer."

Melvin Weinberg, Esq. worked out of a small office on Court Street, in downtown Brooklyn. He made a decent living as a lawyer, after having served twenty years in the NYPD. He loved defending good cops who were getting screwed. The first thing he did was to demand the Medical Examiner's autopsy report on the prisoner. The man was arrested on July 13th, and he died in Bellevue Hospital on July 24th . The cause of death was listed as water on the brain, and pneumonia, followed by the classification as a "criminal homicide." It became apparent that this new Assistant M.E. was out to screw us, and it was time to start circling the wagons.

Lawyer Weinberg made an appointment to see our tormentor, Dr. Bradford V. White, IV, the assistant M.E. who was accusing us of murder or manslaughter. Weinberg was not an imposing figure. He was 5'9", 220 lbs., with balding gray hair, a wrinkled brown suit, yellow shirt, and a cheap flowered tie that looked like some kid at a stand in Coney Island couldn't guess his weight back in 1958.

Dr. White tried to look the part, wearing a seersucker suit and blue and white polka dot bow tie. With his gaunt stature and weak chin, he had a striking resemblance to Ichabod Crane. The young doctor's bow tie was the icing on the cake, and made him look like a total fool. (In Jimmy Kavanaugh's world, it is a near criminal offense for anyone under fifty to wear a bow tie, except with a tuxedo.)

The lawyer got the Assistant M.E. to admit on tape that there were no trauma marks anywhere on the deceased's body. Next on the agenda, was the finding of "water on the brain."

Weinberg bored in. "Doctor White, is it possible that the deceased had water on the brain before his encounter with the police on July 13th, given his bizarre action of pulling a knife on two armed Police Officers?"

"Yes, Mr. Weinberg, it is possible."

"Now, let me ask you this. Is it possible for a police officer, or anyone else, for that matter, to give a man pneumonia, or water on the brain?"

The doctor replied "No, not directly; but it was the extreme irritation of the lungs and brain by the three tear gas canisters that caused his pneumonia and the brain condition."

Weinberg, now smelling blood, came in for the kill. "So, how is it, Doctor, that you are claiming that the responding police officers intentionally, recklessly, or negligently killed the decedent, since you claim this is a criminal homicide?"

Doctor White knew that he was sinking fast, but replied "He was given an overdose of tear gas. They overreacted by using three canisters on him."

"But, Doctor, you were not there, were you?"

"Mr. Weinberg, you know that I was not there."

"Well, Dr. White, can you name any medical text, research, or even a manufacturer's specifications or warnings that tear gas causes water on the brain or pneumonia?"

"Well, ……..no, sir, …..I can not."

"Well, Doctor, before coming to your conclusion as a *criminal homicide,* did you ever contact the manufacturer of the tear gas canisters to see what its side effects are?"

"Well,….no… I didn't."

Weinberg came in for the kill: "I have here the manufacturer's literature on the particular tear gas product. It cannot cause death, only temporary irritation. Basically, its main ingredient is cayenne pepper. So, your entire theory seems to be that the police killed your so-called *homicide victim* with pepper. Maybe you had better go across the street to the A & P and start putting warning labels on the spice rack. You, sir, will be laughed out of the medical profession as a charlatan and a fraud if you proceed with this case as a criminal homicide, or even a homicide. I'll go to Albany and see to it that your medical license is revoked."

Dr. Bradford White, IV was trying to make a name for himself before the annual Medical Examiner's Convention came to town in four weeks. He thought that he could make headlines by having six cops indicted for manslaughter or murder. Dr. White, of course, would be the prosecution's expert witness, and catapult himself to instant fame.

Weinberg, although now a professional man, was still a street cop at heart. He said to the hapless, sputtering M.E., while he bored in again: "Doctor White, I think that you should revise your report, before Sergeant Byrne, Police Officers, Delladonna, Kavanaugh and McInerney, along with the two Emergency Service men, sue you for defamation, and you wind up selling pencils on 34th Street. You are accusing six good men of a serious crime, and I better have your revised report on my desk by 4 P.M. tomorrow. If not, I will personally see to it that you couldn't even get a job checking for the fucking clap in a Tijuana whorehouse!"

Dr. Bradford White, IV, upper class snob, prep school graduate, and Ivy League man, practically shit his pants before the interview was over. His game plan of sacrificing six police officers for his own personal agenda was going down the drain. Worst of all, the tables had been turned on him, and he saw his own career circling the same drain. All of his elitist posturing, his self-important Ivy League superiority and WASP upbringing came crashing down on him, and it was caused by a ballsy Jewish lawyer defending four Irishmen, an Italian, and a Polack. Only in New York!!!!!!

Naturally, Mr. Weinberg received the amended report from Dr. White at about 1:00 P.M. the next day, by messenger. The causes of death were the preexisting conditions of water on the brain and pneumonia, with no mention of homicide.

In New York City government, the walls have ears, and so it was in the office of the Chief Medical Examiner, Dr. Gordon Horowitz. A long time confidant of the Chief told Dr. Horowitz what his assistant, Dr. White, had done. Dr. Horowitz was the premier pathologist in America, and probably the world, and he was somewhat of a police buff at heart. NYPD cops respected Dr. Horowitz, and the feeling was mutual.

The day after attorney Weinberg met with Dr. White, Dr. Horowitz called in the young physician to review the case with him. Horowitz was seething with rage inside, but withheld it well. He was a tall, thin, distinguished looking man in his early sixties, with thinning gray hair, a wispy white mustache, and rimless glasses.

Dr. Horowitz, blunt as ever, said "Dr. White, when you leave 520 First Avenue every day and go out onto the street, do you realize what sort of danger you are in?"

"What do you mean, Dr. Howowitz?"

"Well, once you have left these protected walls, do you realize that your life could be snuffed out in a heartbeat by a lunatic or a criminal? You could wind up as one of those poor souls on the slab in our morgue. The only force protecting you from being transformed from an employed pathologist into some grotesque corpse on the morgue slab is this group of men from the NYPD who you tried to frame with your quasi-medical opinion. In this office, we deal with cold facts and cold cadavers. No political agenda is permitted here.

"Now, I know that you have interacted with Sergeant Byrne's

attorney, Mr. Weinberg. He is a retired NYPD Sergeant, and no fool. Do not lock horns with this man, or his clients. You probably think of yourself as quite superior to working class men, but you are not. While they may not have your advanced degrees, these men are not stupid. When wrongfully accused, they will fight back, and they don't fight fair. Do not use this office ever again to advance your personal political beliefs."

By the end of the interview Dr. Bradford White IV felt so small that he could have parachuted off of a dime, and free-fallen half of the way down.

SELFLESS LOVE

Right after lunch a call came over the air to respond to a basement apartment on East 18th Street, between 2nd and 3rd Avenues. This was a well maintained, tree lined block of brownstones and neat apartment houses. As we pulled up to the five story tenement, we were met by the superintendent and his wife, Mr. and Mrs. Kowalski, a couple in their early seventies. They lived in the basement apartment, a most supers do.

Upon entering the basement apartment we were led over to the kitchen table to a man in a wheelchair, slumped over the table. He had been dead for a while. The Kowalskis explained that this was their 52 year old son, Kevin, who was born with cerebral palsy. Mrs. Kowalski had given Kevin a glass of orange juice, and he just keeled over and died. The pain of their loss had not yet sunk in, and the parents asked us to do C.P.R. to bring their boy back. It was far too late; Kevin was cold to the touch.

I tried to be diplomatic about the fact that there was no procedure that could bring their son back to life. While we were getting the information for our report, the father gave us the heartbreaking family history. He and his wife were married at age nineteen, and a year later they had a son, Kevin, who was born with cerebral palsy. This wonderful couple devoted their entire lives to helping their disabled son for 52 years. They never took a vacation, and were never away from their child for one day. I felt so bad for these people, but I didn't know what to say. What the hell can you say? They called a family member, and we waited for the Medical Examiner to come.

Mr. Kowalski offered us cold sodas, and we sat in the living room chatting. All I could think of was what kind, unselfish, loving people the Kowalskis were. What was wrong with my own father, a violent man, who had four healthy kids and a good wife, and treated them badly? I always suspected that his mistreatment of my brother Frank was the cause of his mental illness.

The Medical Examiner arrived quickly. Luckily, it was not Dr. White. After a brief examination of the deceased, the ruling was "cardiac arrest" and the body was released to the Andrett Funeral Parlor on Second Avenue.

Even many years after retirement, I often thought of the Kowalskis and the selfless devotion to their handicapped son. My heart broke for these wonderful people, but there was nothing I could have done for them, but only to keep them in my thoughts forever. They were the epitome of selfless love. God bless the parents of every handicapped child, and the Mr. and Mrs. Kowalskis of this world. This is the kind of sad memory that most street cops keep in their hearts forever, and only feel comfortable discussing with other cops.

OLD McNALLY GOES TO FARM, E-EYE, E-EYE OH!

Sgt. Kieran McNally was a mean spirited, nasty, abusive drunk. He liked his sauce and used to browbeat younger cops by pulling rank on them. McNally was a tall man, about six feet, three inches, and he had a red face from boozing, that cops call "the Irish sunburn." After the day shift, McNally hit the Anawanda Club and started pumping up pretty good. By 6:00 P.M. he was plastered, and spoiling for a fight.

Tommy and I just brought in a collar for assault and robbery. McNally, now loaded to the gills, came back from the bar and was behind the desk, breathing his beer breath into Lt. Cantorwicz' face. As the Lieutenant was booking our prisoner, Sgt. McNally started to lay into me in a drunken diatribe.

"You think you're some kind of hot shot, don't you, Kavanaugh? Well, you couldn't be a pimple on a good cop's ass, coming in here with a bullshit collar like this. I ought to kick the shit out of you."

Just as the drunken McNally leaned over the desk to hit me, I grabbed him by the lapels of his jacket and began to pull him over the desk. "You want a piece of me, you shanty Irish piece of shit? Let's get it on, you drunken harp! I'll pound your donkey ass into the ground like a fucking human tent peg!"

Uncle Carl knew I was right, but he had to stick up for a fellow boss, to some extent. He grabbed McNally around the waist, and began to pull him back. Now there was a tug of war, with the soused Sergeant as the rope. I backed off out of respect for Lt. Cantorwicz. The Lieutenant ordered McNally to go to the Sergeants' locker room to sleep it off, but McNally could not leave well enough alone.

The building housing the 13th Pct. also contains the Manhattan South Headquarters, responsible for all police operations from 59th Street, down to South Ferry. The building is four stories tall. The Sergeant snuck out of the locker room and began to ride the elevator, pushing the buttons and giggling like the drunken fool he was. He had just taken a dump, and pulled up his boxer shorts to just under his armpits, then pulled up his pants to his waistline. The result was a giddy drunk with about eight inches or more of boxer shorts showing above his belt.

McNally rode the elevator for about fifteen minutes, pushing the buttons and saying things like "B Deck, ladies lingerie, notions and perfume." As he did his routine, the Manhattan South commander, Chief Adam Katzman, got on the elevator and saw this pathetic drunk. The Chief was not amused and immediately went to ream out the desk officer. He stopped short when he realized that it was his own brother-in-law, Carl Cantorwicz. The two men were very close, but the Chief barked out loud "Carl, get this man into rehab now, or he's fired!"

In the 13th Pct. the telephone number for "the farm" was on speed dial. The alcohol program was run by Monsignor Francis Dunphy, the Catholic chaplain. He had a goon squad of dried-out-drunks who kidnapped the *patients* and brought them to the farm in upstate New York. The Monsignor's men came quickly and snapped up McNally, who had been to the farm before. As Yogi Berra might have said "It was 'déjà vu' all over again." Lt. Cantorwicz was glad to see him go, because another problem had been avoided.

IT'S A WRAP!

About 8:00 P.M. on a weekday night we were called to a swanky apartment house at 75 Fifth Avenue, apartment 10-C. The call was vague: "investigate suspicious condition in the apartment."

We arrived promptly and announced ourselves to the doorman, a young, early twenties *greenhorn,* with a very thick brogue, right off of the boat from Ireland.

When going into an apartment house, veteran cops know enough to give the doorman due respect and tell him where they are going, unless they suspect that the occupant will be tipped off. Young cops, in their misplaced machismo, barge right past the doorman, ignoring someone whom they incorrectly perceive to be a lowly figure.

We told the doorman that we got a call to 10-C, and asked him if he could give us some information about the tenant. Any time you want to know what's going on in a neighborhood, always ask a bartender or a doorman. You'll usually get the straight scoop.

This case proved no differently. Young Liam Comerford, from County Longford, told us that the man in apartment 10-C was a certifiable whack job, always complaining about space ships and aliens following him, and things like that. I was glad that we got our briefing before going up.

The man answering the bell was well dressed, late forties, and a smoker. He held a lit cigarette in a holder, which to me usually meant the guy was either filthy rich, gay, putting on airs, or maybe all of the above. He wore a black silk smoking jacket, and was obviously a man with a lot of money.

Tommy introduced us and asked him what the problem was.

"Well", said Herbert Tunnington, "I've lived here for ten years. Since last year my neighbors on both sides have been shooting invisible rays into my apartment, trying to give me cancer."

After twenty seconds of listening to this man it was quite apparent that he was nutty as a shithouse rat. The difference between a psycho and an eccentric is that the latter has money. Tunnington was, of course, a raving eccentric.

We stroked the guy off real good. We inspected the walls for cracks, checked out the ceilings and plumbing. Our recommendation to Mr. Tunnington was that he obtain a large quantity of aluminum foil and paper his walls with it, with the shiny side facing his neighbors. That way, the rays will bounce off and give them cancer, instead of him. Tommy even made a tinfoil hat for him to wear in the apartment, to protect his brain from the rays. Mr. Tunnington was thrilled with this solution, and he tried to give us $50.00 each, which we graciously declined, but really desired.

MATERNITY MADNESS

Back on the day tour the day was going quickly for the east side sectors, and the west side was also hopping. About 3:30 P.M. we were on East 15th Street and First Avenue and looking forward to getting off work in half an hour. The dispatcher was trying to get a west side sector to go on a maternity call at the Stamford Arms Hotel at 155 West 22nd Street, between 6th and 7th Avenues. Nobody was responding, probably because the Stamford Arms was a sleazy hotel, filled with roaches, rats, huge water bugs, and a sleazy clientele of winos, junkies, hookers, and welfare recipients.

Since we were on First Avenue, I said to Tommy "I'll be dipped in shit if we're going all the way over there. It's nothing but skells in that fuckin' place."

We were about to be dipped in shit as the dispatcher called 13 Adam-Boy to respond to the maternity call at the Stamford Arms Hotel, room 5G. We reluctantly took the job from Central, as Tommy slammed down the mike.

We had to buck traffic westbound on 23rd Street all the way to 7th Avenue. The hotel was just east of 7th Avenue, and we finally arrived. There was no ambulance on the scene. I was hoping that it took us so long to get there that the ambulance had come and gone. As we entered the dingy lobby, we were met by the desk clerk who had a room temperature I.Q. We told him that we had a maternity call in Room 5G. The idiot didn't know what a maternity case was, and I didn't have time to explain it to him.

Knocking on the door to room 5G, we were let in by the proud father, a guy about forty-five, who had obviously lost something off of his mental fastball over the years. The small room, with peeling, piss-yellow paint, was dimly lit by one 20 watt light bulb dangling from a single electric wire in the middle of the ceiling.

On the bed lay an obese black woman, in her late thirties, who was writhing in pain. "What's the matter, ma'am" Tommy asked.

"I thinks I's pregnant, officuh."

"What makes you think you're pregnant?" asked McInerney.

"I ain't got my period fo' about five o' six month, and I feels real funny insides, ya' know" was her response.

Well, with all the triage and medical history being put aside, this *baby mama* reared back and yelled "MUTHA-FUCKA-SHEEEEEEEEEET!!!" then squirted out a seven month premature baby girl onto the mattress, in one huge, wet, fart-like blast. We were completely dumbfounded for a few seconds, then quickly recovered. The little girl showed no signs of life, and she was apparently stillborn.

This was all new to Tommy, so I asked him to get a towel to hold the baby in. Seconds felt like hours, and I picked up the slippery, lifeless child in the towel. She was a preemie, weighing only two or three pounds. I noticed that her mouth was clogged with amniotic fluid, so I used my finger to clear her airway. I gently shook her, then smacked her butt; however, the child still showed no signs of life. Just at the moment I was going to tell the mother that the child was stillborn, the baby started crying. I felt that a huge burden had been lifted off of my shoulders. It was great to be a life saver, rather than a life taker, even considering the seedy surroundings.

The fifth floor of the low rent hotel was filled with society's losers, but they cheered us for saving the child. We called again for the ambulance, but they were not coming any time soon. Act two was about to come. The child had been delivered, but was still attached to the umbilical cord. So, here I was, holding onto this little screaming preemie and thinking of a way to cut the cord so that the child would not bleed out into the placenta and die. Tommy knocked on some doors and found an elderly woman who knitted. He got a couple of feet of yarn from her, and borrowed her scissors.

Mom went into contractions again and blasted out the placenta onto the bed in a giant "WHOOOOSSSSH." The onlookers were grossed out. After giving the baby to the mother to hold, I couldn't wait any longer. Saying to myself, "Fuck it", I tied the cord in two places, about eight inches apart, then cut the cord in the middle with the scissors, and hoped for the best.

About ten minutes later an ambulance came and took the mother and child to St. Vincent's Hospital. By now, I was covered with baby muck and blood, and just wanted to go back to the station house to clean up. When we got four blocks from the Precinct, we heard a call of a burglary in progress at 226 East 17th Street, top floor apartment. The suspect was a male black, with a blue shirt.

Realizing that we were right around the corner, Tommy wheeled around and we were there in fifteen seconds. We raced in and were informed that the suspect had fled up the fourth floor scuttle stairs to the roof. On the fourth floor landing, we found the burglar's wallet, which contained his Riker's Island I.D card.

As soon as we got on the roof we were met by an irate neighbor, who said "What the hell were you doing, eating donuts? I called 15 minutes ago."

I had my back to her, and turned around showing my arms, face, and torso covered with blood, and said "Not exactly, ma'am, I was delivering a baby."

She ran off, humiliated. "Fuck you, you snotty rich bitch", I muttered to myself.

DETECTIVE FREDDIE ZARULLO

After washing up, we went to the Detective Squad on the second floor. The detective on duty was Freddie Zarullo, one of the most lethargic men ever to serve as an NYPD detective. Zarullo wasn't a bad guy, but he was not motivated, to put it mildly. Freddie was the product of a Spanish father and an Armenian mother. He had great ability as an investigator, but he tried to shit-can nearly every case he had. Freddie's trademark was chain smoking Lucky Strikes with no filters, and he wore a snappy gray fedora, looking like a half-assed detective in a 1940's Hollywood B movie.

We presented our case to Detective Zarullo and went over the whole story of just missing the burglar, and finding his wallet that he lost in the escape. Reflexively, Freddie went into his tap dancing routine, saying "Look guys, the man is just going to say he lost his wallet on the subway. This is a bull-shit case, and we'll never get a conviction."

Overhearing everything was Freddie's boss, Sergeant Walter Herring. He was an outstanding detective supervisor, and not one to tolerate Freddie's act. The Sergeant came up to Zarullo and said "Freddie, it's Friday afternoon. If you don't have a collar on this case by Monday, you're transferred."

There was no love lost between the two men. Sergeant Herring once told Zarullo "Freddie, you couldn't find a Jew in Miami Beach, in the middle of fucking winter."

Freddie, now properly chastised, went into action. Without leaving his desk, he called Riker's Island and found out that his suspect was released from jail at 10:00 A.M. that morning. They gave Freddie the burglar's telephone number in the Bronx. At 4:00

P.M. Zarullo called the burglar's house and left a message with his mother, stating that he found her son's wallet, and he wanted to return it to him.

At 5:30 P.M., the burglar, Jamal Wiggins, came into the 13th Pct. Detective Squad to see Freddie. He had a major attitude and said that he lost his wallet that morning. The moron was still wearing the same blue shirt that he wore during the burglary. Zarullo told him that his fingerprints were found all over the apartment, which was a baldfaced lie. Wiggins confessed to the burglary right then and there. Freddie got "on the sheet" with a good felony collar, and the lazy bastard never left his chair, which further pissed off Sgt. Herring to no end.

GARDEN VARIETY WEIRDO

We were always busy on the 4 to 12 shift. We had bounced all over the command this evening, from the east side to the west, and north to south. There were only four radio cars running in the whole precinct, instead of nine, as a result of the layoffs. Around 11:00 P.M. we got a call to a penthouse apartment on East 18th Street, between 1st and 2nd Avenues. The dispatcher's communication merely said "See if ambulance is needed."

Upon ringing the bell, we were met by a man in his mid-fifties, bent over slightly at the waist, and in obvious pain. He was naked, save for the white towel around his waist. The man looked like someone had just kicked him square in the balls.

Tommy asked "What's the matter with you?"

He responded " Look, gentlemen, please don't laugh, but I have a serious problem, and it's very embarrassing. Can I confide in you boys?"

I said, "Don't worry, sir, we'll do our best to help you. There's nobody from the Police Department who is going to hurt you in any way." (I couldn't use the line *"We're professional police officers"* any more after the *Pickle Puss* incident, without laughing in the guy's face).

The man was a big player on Wall Street named Brice Baron Mac Intosh. The working class, Irish-German-Catholic antennae in me went up whenever I encountered a wealthy WASP like this. My internal *"This prick will fuck you in a goddam minute"* radar was put on full alert. However, my suspicions were for naught.

"O.K., You seem like two men I can trust to help me. You see, my problem is ……..my problem is …. that I have a…… a… ten inch carrot...... stuck up my ass."

This was a new one for us. We thought that we had seen it all, but this was tops. I was going to ask the guy how it happened, but sort of figured it out all by myself. He must have been giving himself a vegan prostate massage, overdid it a bit, and lost his grip on the carrot when he began "whipping his skippy." There was no sense in embarrassing the man any further by requesting an ambulance, just to go two blocks to the Cabrini Medical Center. So, we decided to take him there in the radio car.

I looked over at McInerney and could tell that my partner was chuckling inside, but holding it in. We sure as hell didn't need another *Pickle Puss* incident in our folders. Tommy, however, just could not resist asking the man "What the hell were you trying to do, Mr. Mac Intosh, improve your hindsight?"

With that quip, Mac Intosh, Tommy and I went in convulsions, laughing hysterically. Carrot Ass fell to his knees and laughed so hard that his vegetable suppository quickly dislodged itself and squirted out onto his expensive red, green and white Oriental rug, which probably cost more than two years of my salary.

I sure as hell wasn't picking up that carrot. There are limits to the term "public servant." Tommy, always available with a smart remark, said to the guy "Well, sir, there's no charge for the house call."

The physically and emotionally relieved man was so ecstatic over relieving his alimentary ailment that he told us "You officers really saved me from some major embarrassment. I'd like to have you boys over for dinner sometime."

McInerney was quick to chime in "Thanks, for the invitation, Mac, but you can hold the fucking salad, because I ain't eating it."

Mac Intosh laughed so hard that he collapsed onto his couch and could not show us to the door, so we let ourselves out of the penthouse. When Tommy gave the disposition to the dispatcher, he tersely stated: "condition corrected."

BUTCHER BOY

The layoffs brought some very different people together. They say that politics make strange bedfellows, well, so does the layoff of cops. Police Officer Fred Davidovich, known as 'Mr. Wizard', had found his niche in the 13th Pct. with his new partner, Jack Van Pelt. Jack, simply called "Van" in the Precinct, got transferred from the Bronx Emergency Service Unit. Van Pelt was a long time Emergency cop. When the layoff roster came out, it was either Jack or the Captain's nephew going back to patrol. Jack lost that one, so now he and Mr. Wizard were joined at the hip as radio car partners in sectors 13 Eddie-Frank, in the middle of the Precinct.

One July afternoon a horrible call came over the radio. Hector Matos was a local teenager who worked for Pete the Butcher on 3rd Avenue near East 21std Street, right around the corner from the Precinct. Hector did odd jobs and deliveries. Pete also used Hector to make chop meat and always had to remind the kid to push the meat in with a block of wood, instead of using his hand.

Hector was not going to win a Nobel Prize for physics any time soon, and would always forget to use the wooden block. While Pete was in the back inspecting a new delivery of beef, Hector was up front, making chop meat, and failed to use the wooden block, as usual. Pete heard his worker's agonized scream and came forward to see Hector's hand being forcibly drawn into the meat grinder. By the time Pete managed to pull the plug on the machine, Hector's hand was lost up to the wrist. Pete called 911 in a panic. He could hardly speak to the operator.

Sgt. Byrne and Danny Delladonna had just left the station house, when they heard the call. They were less than a block away.

81

When they came into the store, Hector was screaming loudly, and they saw that his arm was trapped in the stainless steel meat grinder. Hector's blood was pouring from the machine, and the kid was bleeding to death. What used to be his hand lay in a heap on the brown butcher block, in a pool of blood and ground up flesh and bone. Since they couldn't dislodge his arm from the grinder, Sgt. Byrne quickly applied a tourniquet to Hector's arm. They called for Emergency Service, but were advised that there were no units available. Due to the layoffs, there was only one Emergency truck in all of Manhattan South.

Danny Delladonna quickly reminded the Sergeant that Davidovich and Van Pelt were working as sectors 13 Eddie-Frank. Sergeant's chauffeurs, like Danny D, were a great asset to the NYPD patrol force. They were usually older men who were a wealth of information for the younger boss, who appreciated the advice that the veteran officer could quietly give them on the side. Danny Delladonna was such a man.

Sgt. Byrne asked the dispatcher to have sector Eddie-Frank respond to the location forthwith.

Van Pelt and Davidovich were on 5th Avenue and 21st Street when they got the call. Van, a terrific driver, got there in under two minutes. They quickly sized up the problem. Davidovich initially considered taking the machine apart to free the kid's hand, but rejected it as too time consuming, given the circumstances. If the tourniquet were left on too long, the boy's arm might be lost. If it were taken off, the kid would bleed to death.

When we arrived, Hector was screaming in agony, as anyone who had just had his hand turned into a bloody mound of ground chuck would normally do. Delladonna gave the boy some soothing words: "Shut the fuck up, kid!"

Mr. Wizard's mind was racing for a solution, and he found one. He went into his tool bag and took the back cover off the meat grinder to expose the wiring. Davidovich reversed the polarity and asked Sgt. Byrne to plug the machine in, all the while thinking

82

"This will either work, or take this dumb bastard's arm off up to the fucking elbow."

With the machine plugged in, and the polarity reversed, Sgt. Byrne turned the machine on. As expected, the grinder reversed itself and released its death grip on Hector's arm. The sight of the boy's bloody stump was horrifying. A towel was quickly put on his wound, and he was rushed off to Bellevue, with our car running interference for the ambulance.

At home that evening, I said to myself, over and over, that I will never, never, ever, buy chop meat from Pete ever again. I didn't care if he marinated that grinder in Clorox for a week and a half.

For Jack Van Pelt, this brought back painful memories from three years before when he was an Emergency Service cop in the Bronx. He received a call to go to a meat packing plant near the Bronx Terminal Market where two brothers were cleaning a huge meat grinder, the kind used to grind up a whole steer. One brother climbed into the machine, and while inside, his foot hit the safety release and started the machine. He suffered the fate of every cow that ever went through that grinder, while his brother watched helplessly in total horror. Most of the man's body was ground up, until the machine got stuck on his cowboy boots. Jack and his partner were the first cops on the scene, and he suffered a mental breakdown over it. He was out of work for over two months.

Every big city cop has that one incident that is locked away in his memory bank forever, only to come out unexpectedly from time to time, and haunt him for the rest of his life. I had mine from my days as a foot cop in Greenwich Village.

Van Pelt was not a daily drinker, and rarely did he stop at the Anawanda Club after work, like the rest of us did. He usually went straight home to his house in Glendale, Queens. This night, Van Pelt went to the Anawanda and got stewed. He was not a good drinker, and the events of the day brought back some very dark and horrifying memories for him.

Van was an avid reader who read one book a week. The last

thing that he read that night, as he knelt on the floor, puking his guts out and hugging the toilet bowl in the men's room of the Anawanda Club, was:

"SLOAN VALVE COMPANY, CHIGAGO, ILLINOIS."

THANKS FOR THE LIGHT!

Quaranta and Malloy had just finished a job at Metropolitan Life at 23rd and Madison, and were heading back east. As they drove along 23rd Street, they heard female screams for help. A young thief had approached an elderly woman from behind, and tried to take her purse. The victim, a Hispanic woman in her seventies, fought back and was knocked down by the robber. Not content with just getting her purse, the low-life stomped in her face, and then broke her arm.

As the cops approached in the radio car, the robber ran off toward Park Avenue South with the victim's pocketbook in hand. He was running like a ghetto gazelle. The guy was a true perp in that he wore Pro Keds, known to cops as "felony shoes." They followed the robber and saw him go down into the subway. As expected, he vaulted over the turnstile, and headed toward the platform. Quaranta cursed every cigarette he ever had, and Malloy every beer, as they tried to keep up with the young criminal. Incredibly, the suspect jumped onto the tracks. They took a quick look and saw that no train was coming, so down they went into the subway, the dark abyss that cops call "the hole." Both men were scared shitless, but kept up the chase anyway.

The little wise-ass was gaining on them, and he would turn around and smirk every now and then at the two older cops trying to arrest him. As the smug little bastard turned around once more, laughing at his pursuers, he stumbled on one of the railroad ties, and fell to his left. To break his fall, he reached out and grabbed the third rail with both hands. He was instantly zapped by 660 volts of electricity. Within a few seconds the young punk was in the kneeling position and sizzling like a porterhouse steak. He would soon be on fire, head to toe.

As Terry retrieved the victim's pocketbook, Sabu pulled up, huffing and puffing, just in time to see the smoldering corpse of what was a living human being just moments before. He reflexively took out his pack of Marlboros, pulled out a cigarette and held it up to the burning cadaver. Lighting his butt off the blazing corpse's shirt, he said: "Thanks for the light, cocksucker."

Before Vinny could take a second drag on his Marlboro, the unmistakable sound of a subway train bearing down on them in the black, dank tunnel terrified both cops.

Shining his flashlight, Sabu found a slight bow in the wall, and they latched themselves onto it like two patches of moss. The train whizzed past the two cops in what seemed like an hour, but was only a few seconds.

Malloy was the first to speak "Vinny, I think I shit myself. Are we dead or alive?"

Quaranta was so scared that he felt like his balls were up in his neck. When he could finally recover his voice, he said, "Christ, I don't know, Terry, I never died before."

The two cops stood in the middle of the train tracks patting themselves all over, looking for signs of blood and lost limbs. Meanwhile, the purse snatcher was ground into bits by ten cars of the subway train. The largest piece of him could have fit into a shoe box.

By the end of the summer, the *layoff cops*, as we came to be known, would get used to it. Because there were so many hospitals in the Precinct, there were frequent subway jumpers. Someone would get a bad diagnosis and told they had a terminal illness, and on the way home they'd take the shortcut to heaven by jumping in front of a moving subway. Then the NYPD would get to pick up the pieces.

REVENGE ON NURSE RATCHED

Cops and nurses are kindred spirits. Due to the nature of their work, they interact a lot. There is just something in a nurse's outfit that is a natural aphrodisiac to cops. Patrol cops are in and out of the Emergency Rooms on a daily basis, and get along with the hospital staff and the ambulance EMT's. They know enough when to defer to medical personnel, and they understand the E.R.'s rules. The nurses and doctors know that if they are ever in trouble, the cops will be there in no time.

Just before we were to break for lunch, the dispatcher called out "In the 13th Precinct, a man stabbed in Stuyvesant Park."

We took the call and quickly sped down Second Avenue to East 15th Street. The victim was a well dressed white man lying on his back, semi-conscious. This guy was way out of his element. He was bleeding profusely from a deep knife wound. As it turned out, he was a salesman from Maryland who went to the park to buy marijuana. The junkies made him as an easy mark, and tried to rob him. He fought back, and for his efforts, he was stabbed twice: Once on the arm, and once in the chest. Tommy ripped his shirt open to expose the wound; it was oozing bubbles, which indicated a sucking chest wound, where the lung was punctured. In these cases, it is very important to create an airtight seal over the wound.

"Tommy, give me the cellophane off of your cigarette pack," I said.

With that, I placed the cellophane over the bubbling wound and pressed down. The ambulance arrived in no time and took the man to Cabrini Medical Center. Upon arriving, the EMT's, Tommy and I took the injured man into the Emergency Room, and straight to a treatment room. We had apparently violated charge nurse Margaret McBride's shrill admonition to stop at the front desk, fill out the patient's admission form, and provide the insurance information. Forget that the poor bastard was dying, just fill out the paperwork first. No wonder her nickname was *Nurse Ratched.*

Predictably, Nurse Ratched lashed out at us about our violation of hospital protocol. I ignored it, feeling that she just had a bug up her ass, but Tommy did not take such criticism lightly. He replied to her "Look, Nurse Ratched, we have a man here with a sucking chest wound. Save the man's life first, then get his Blue Cross card later."

Ratched was pissed. "We have rules here, officer, and they are to be obeyed at all times. And please remember that my name is McBride, not Ratched!"

I felt that this was one broad who needed to get laid, real bad.

Tommy was still seething about the treatment we received. I told him "She's new here, Tommy. After a while, she'll get with it. Just ignore her."

"Fuck her, Jimmy. I know how to handle a bitch like this. She needs to be taught a lesson", as he turned the radio car southbound on Third Avenue, heading south until it became The Bowery.

The Bowery was rife with winos and stumblebum drunks. We found a sleeping bum, and took his full bottle of Ripple, a cheap muscatel wine. After making a U-turn, we came upon an older bum, who was nodding off in a sitting position, leaning against a boarded-up building. He looked like someone's grandfather who had not shaved for a month, and had been pissing in his pants for just as long. His acrid body odor burned our nostrils.

This was Tommy's party, and he did all of the talking. He approached the old wino and said "Hey, Pop, do you want to make some money and get cleaned up? You'll also get a free bottle of Ripple."

The old geezer's eyes lit up. "You bet your ass, officer. What do

88

I have to do?"

Tommy said "Just get in the back seat, Pop, and on the way up Third Avenue we'll tell you what to do."

When we got about forty feet from the Emergency Room of Cabrini Medical Center, Tommy gave him a $5 bill. He pointed to E.R. door and said "Now go in there, and tell the tall nurse with the black hair (McBride) that you have bad pains in your stomach, and you haven't taken a crap in about two or three weeks. When you get out, there will be a bottle of Ripple for you, right here, hidden in this bed of ivy."

All went as planned, and Nurse Ratched wound up, not only having to give the bum an enema, but she also gave him a shower as her punishment. The other nurses knew what was going on and loved it.

Tommy spent the rest of the day grinning like a Cheshire cat. He wondered out loud what type of payback was better. Was it the kind where the victim doesn't realize they'd been had, like Nurse Ratched, or, like Sgt. Nordstrom, where they know they've been fucked?

WILD KINGDOM

Our Precinct was the largest in Manhattan, and went all the way from the East River, west to Seventh Avenue. As you went west of Fifth Avenue, the area became more industrial, and less residential. Some adventuresome people moved into the old factories, called lofts, and established residences there. The places were not bad once they were fixed up. Many units had fifteen foot high ceilings. This type of living attracted some weird types who liked to keep exotic animals in their lofts, the kind that were not quite suited for Manhattan apartment living.

Sgt. "Wild Bill" Hanley was taken off the midnight shift by Capt. Fitzgerald, as punishment for drinking, and put on the day shift, where he could be monitored more closely. Hanley whined for weeks about not getting the night differential pay, so the Captain put him on the 4 to 12 shift, figuring that the fast pace and heavy work load would keep him too busy to drink. Also, his driver was "Big Jim" Galligan, a former paratrooper, whose job it was to keep Wild Bill on the straight and narrow path. At 6:45 P.M. we got a call to investigate an "animal condition" in a loft on the 8th floor of 935 Broadway. Idiot Hanley chimed in that he was also going. "That's all we need, that asshole coming to look over our shoulders," I blurted out.

It was probably a barking dog, or something like that, I thought. When we pulled up, Sgt. Hanley and Big Jim were waiting for us in front of a seventy five year old building with faded brown bricks that was once a factory. New York's high taxes and unions forced most of these industrial shops to relocate to the southern states.

The elevator was not working, so the four of us hoofed it up

90

eight flights of stairs. As we approached the eighth floor, there was a terrible odor. Galligan knocked on the door, and a thin, pasty faced white man with a pony tail and a *go fuck yourself* look on his face opened the door just a crack. Upon seeing the four cops, he got cocky and said in a *Noo Yawk* accent "Whatayah wan'?"

Hanley told him "We were sent here to investigate an animal condition. Do you have any animals in your apartment, sir?"

The tenant started to tap dance, and Big Jim said "Your place smells like a zoo. I know you've got an animal in there. Let's see it!"

With that, the tenant swung the door wide open and a male lion came running at us, growling like the MGM Studio mascot. Galligan quickly grabbed the door and slammed it shut, as we rushed out of the apartment and regrouped on the seventh floor landing, staring down at the one inch square, dingy white tiles, in semi-shock.

At first, Hanley thought that he was having the D.T.'s, because he had not had a drink in two days, and thought that he was having hallucinations. We looked at each other as if to say "Did you see what I thought we saw?" The consensus was that we had seen a real lion in the apartment, a young, male lion.

The four of us went back up to the loft and knocked on the door again. Mr. Pony Tail opened the door a bit, and he had a shit-eating grin on his face, figuring that the cops would leave him alone now. Hanley told him that he had a dangerous animal in the apartment, and he must restrain it. The lion was tied up and we entered the loft. The owner had an eight foot square litter box filled with sawdust that was the source of the odor throughout the building.

Big Jim tried talking to the guy and asked him why he would have such an animal in the city. The man told Galligan that ever since he was a kid he always loved wild animals. He was very upset that somehow his pet boa constrictor got out of the loft the week before and couldn't be found.

After the Emergency Service cops came and tranquilized the

lion, it was taken to the Bronx Zoo, and the owner was given a Health Code summons for keeping an exotic, dangerous animal within New York City limits. Hanley, ever the great sage, said to the tenant on the way out "Why don't you just get a dog, like everyone else?"

A few days later, an unsuspecting neighbor found nature boy's boa constrictor in her bedroom when she came home from work. It has traversed the heating ducts and came into her loft. The woman screamed so loudly that she was heard in the next building.

HEARTBREAK AT BICKFORD'S

We were back on the midnight shift, and the night was going by quickly. As soon as we finished one job, Central gave us another. After a brief lull, a call came over of a man stabbed at Bickford's, 7th Avenue and West 14th Street.

Sector George-Henry-Ida was only two blocks away and got there in seconds. We arrived a minute later. A large crowd surrounded a 19 year old man and a hooker. The prostitute had stabbed the man after he had made a perceived insult to the three hookers sitting across the counter from him. There was no mistaking the girls for prostitutes, given their slutty attire. Their tits were popping out of their tank tops, and they had short shorts which exposed half of their asses.

All the kid said to them was "You girls working tonight?"

One hooker, Daisy Kane, got so insulted at being made for a prostitute that she pulled out a knife and threatened to stab the young man, named Emil Sikorski, from Wilkes-Barre, Pennsylvania. Emil was visiting his aunt, and did odd jobs in the neighborhood for the summer.

Emil picked up a sugar shaker and prepared to hit the bimbo with it, and she backed off. Believing that the incident was over, the young man continued to sip his coffee. As the three girls got up to leave, Daisy pulled out her knife again, and stabbed the unsuspecting Sikorski square in the chest.

Unfortunately for Emil, it was a one in a million jab, because the knife went in between his ribs, and nicked his aorta. Although he was up and talking, he was a walking dead man, who was slowly bleeding to death internally.

Sky King and The Admiral took Emil to St. Vincent's Emergency Room, only three blocks away. Within five minutes of arriving at the hospital, the attending physician came out and told Podolsky and Mulligan that Emil Sikorski was dead. They were stunned for the moment, then realized that a routine assault was now a homicide. They quickly relayed a radio message to us to hold Daisy Kane. However, we already had her in cuffs. If fact, after we read her the Miranda rights, Daisy led us to the dumpster where she put the bloody knife. She identified the knife as hers, and confessed that she just wanted to scare the kid for insulting her.

I just didn't get the whole thing. A broad who worked as a prostitute, and dressed the part, got irate when she was 'off-duty', because a man recognized her as a hooker.

It was my turn up, and I took the collar. It was very unusual for a uniformed police officer to make an arrest for murder. Most killers don't wait around for the cops to come.

Daisy Kane was easily indicted for murder, after Chester Podolsky and I testified, along with the Emergency Room doctor, the night manager from Bickford's, and her two hooker friends.

In the fall, the trial preparation with the Manhattan District Attorney's Office would be an incredibly heartbreaking experience for me, since I had to meet with Emil's parents. There are no words of condolence you can give a parent who has lost a child, especially in a homicide. Daisy would eventually cop a plea to Manslaughter Second Degree, and was sentenced to nine years in prison.

I could offer no explanation to the distraught parents for such a low sentence.

AN "UDDER" DELIGHT

The late tour brings out many strange characters who wander into a Manhattan police station. The 13th Precinct was no exception. There was the Elvis impersonator who would stand in front of the desk singing and playing his guitar for hours, until the desk officer finally had it and kicked him out. The ersatz Elvis had a voice that sounded like Andy Devine after he gargled with razor blades and iodine.

Another regular was the out of work comedian, Joey D., who did celebrity voice impersonations. He was my favorite. This guy could do every politician, actor and singer. From time to time he worked in small clubs, but he suffered from stage fright. So Joey D. would practice his act in the station house in front of a friendly audience.

Loretta was a short, fat, red-head who walked around with three or four dogs. She would come into the station house with the dogs, and talk for hours, to no one in particular. She loved to initiate new cops to the Precinct by coming up to them and grabbing them by the dick and balls and say: "How's your hammer hanging, Johnny?"

"Crazy Eddie" was a harmless old fool, about 65, who came in a couple of times a week. It was rumored that he was once an electrical engineer who had a mental breakdown. Eddie wore a filthy trench coat that had dozens of alligator clips attached to it. He would come into the station house and greet the desk officer by saying "Nice to see you, Loo", about twenty or thirty times. Then he would babble on for hours, talking to himself , or anyone who would listen, about the current events of the world, until he got tired and left, or the desk officer told him enough was enough.

"Skateboard Sammy" was a man in his twenties who was born with only half a body. He had no legs, but had a normal size trunk and head. He made his living by begging at the E. 23rd Street subway station. Sammy made his way around the city on a contraption that looked like a large skateboard. He liked to come into the station house and mooch cigarettes from the cops, and hang out and bullshit for hours. Despite his lack of legs, Sammy had massive arm strength, and would lift himself off of the skateboard, and hoist himself onto the desk, where he would badger the Desk Officer for a cigar or a cigarette.

This night, Lt. Carl Cantorwicz was on the desk, smoking his usual cigar. Next to him was Sammy, perched on the desk, also smoking a cigar that he grubbed from Uncle Carl. The switchboard operator was civilian, Winnie McKinley. Winnie was an old-timer who was a surrogate sister to the cops in the Precinct. She knew what to say to the wives when the boys were around the corner at the Anawanda Club. This night would be no different, as some more regulars came in around 2:00 A.M There were three transvestites who lived next door to the Precinct: Peaches, Laverne and Shirley. These were men who dressed as women. They had the surgery to augment their breasts, but did not have their genitalia removed. As cops would say, "the carpet didn't match the drapes."

Laverne had the most beautiful breasts money could buy, and she loved to expose them in public. Whenever Uncle Carl had the desk, Laverne and her entourage would come in after bar hopping and they'd go into their routine. Laverne would lift up her blouse and expose her silicone 44 triple D's. Then she would stand behind the Lieutenant and wedge his bald head between her huge tits, then wiggle around. Winnie had seen the act so many times before that she didn't even look up. Carl was a widower and appreciated the attention, no matter the source.

This night, Laverne and her gang came in, and she started doing her act, first with Sammy, and then with Carl. As fate would have it, a family from Nebraska was driving to Manhattan for vacation, and were lost. They were looking for the Gramercy Park Hotel, just two blocks away from the Precinct. Seeing the green lights of the police station, the family got out and went inside to ask for directions. In came the four Corn Huskers: mom, dad, the 8 year old boy, and 6 year old girl.

It was a sight to behold. There was Laverne, with her huge, *beaudacious* knockers wrapped around Uncle Carl's bald head, with a cigar sticking out of his mouth. Sammy, the half of a man, was sitting on the desk, smoking one of Carl's cigars, all the while sucking on the teat of one of the other "girls." The parents were aghast and speechless, and the little boy blurted out "Mommy, what's that lady doing to the policeman?"

WARRANT MAN

Tommy's father had died and was being waked in Queens. The job gave you four days off when you had a death in the immediate family. This left me without a partner for a few days. Captain Fitzgerald had just received a poor evaluation in one area – clearing up arrest warrants – so he was hell bent to correct it.

Capt. Fitz called me and Al Jackson into his office. He handed us a stack of about forty warrants and said "I want three a night. I don't care what you do after that."

I had only done patrol duty, and had never served arrest warrants. Basically, if someone was arrested and let go on bail for his next court appearance, then failed to show up, the judge would issue an arrest warrant. It was the job of the Precinct Warrant Officer to bring him in. Our "Warrant Man" had been laid off on July 1st.

Al Jackson spent his entire career up to now in Harlem Precincts. His last position was as a homicide investigator in the Sixth Homicide Division. Al was an outwardly humorous man, but inside he was bitter about having never received the gold detective's shield that he greatly deserved. Still, Jackson came in every day, worked hard, and was recognized by everyone as a great cop. We got along well, having been together at the Max' Kansas City brawl. There was a good bond between us, although we came from much different backgrounds. We would also be working in plainclothes.

My partner for the next few nights was very experienced at serving warrants. The first order of priority was to sort out the warrants by address. Al saw that eight of the wanted men were all from the same single room occupancy hotel, so we started out there.

The warrants all had the defendants' photos on them, so we knew who we were looking for. Nearly all of the suspects were black. Al knew that I was from Staten Island, so he said "Jimmy, just let me do all of the talking when we get there, O.K.?"

"You got it, partner. I'll be right behind you, like a mute" I said.

We pulled up near the Bellemore Hotel on Lexington and twenty-eighth. It was a low-life place, filled with criminals, whores, junkies, and other of life's failures. The desk clerk was a career criminal, and could not be trusted. After identifying ourselves, we walked up the stairs so he wouldn't know where we were heading.

The first man we were trying to find was named Alonzo Jones. Jackson knocked on the door and said "**POH**-leece! Open up!"

The splintered door opened a bit, and the man inside said "*Who yo lookin' fo', officah?*"

Jackson said "I'm looking for James Green." Relieved, the occupant said "There's nobody here by that name."

So Jackson asked "So, what's *your* name?"

The incredibly stupid man said "I'm Alonzo Jones."

With one quick push of the door, the broad shouldered Jackson pushed his way into the room and handcuffed the man. The place smelled like a hamper full of dirty socks and a quart of toe jams.

Out of earshot of the prisoner, Al instructed me in the ways of the ghetto. "Jimmy, whenever you're dealing with a street nigger, you never tell the man that you are looking for him. Always say that you are looking for someone else. That way, the he will be so happy that you don't want *him*, that he'll give up his real name right away. Also, whenever you knock on the guy's door, don't say 'POLICE! You have to say "**POH**-LEECE!', otherwise, they won't open the door for you."

I was taken aback with the raw racial bluntness of my partner, but I received some valuable lessons in police work that evening. By arrest number three, Al even let me do the talking. When we got in the room to make the third collar, there was another man present. Jackson recognized the man, and sure enough, we had a warrant for him, too. We got a *two fer* out of it. Captain Fitzgerald was ecstatic about the four arrests we brought in that night.

After taking the prisoners to the Manhattan jail, known as The Tombs, I spent the rest of the night working out in the Police Academy gym, and topped it off with a swim in the pool. Being a former staff member, I still had the keys to the place. The next two days with Jackson was just like the first. But, by day four, the collars got harder to make. It seemed like the wanted people knew the cops were coming. Nobody would open the door for us, so Al would have to improvise. He carried an old briefcase with him. In it, he had a syringe, the size of which a veterinarian would use on a horse, along with a jar of a very foul smelling liquid. It smelled like a mixture of skunk's spray and horse manure, but was ten times worse.

At the Hotel 21, at 21 East 21st Street, we knew the wanted man was in the room, but he would not open up at all. The hotel owners got pissed off if we kicked the doors in, and it wasn't worth being hassled over the petty civilian complaints. So, Al took his syringe, filled it with his magic potion, and squirted it under the suspect's door. Within less than a minute the man came out, gasping for fresh air. The other two fared no better that night.

I admired Al's resourcefulness and knowledge of criminals. I said to myself "This man is one hell of a cop."

KEEPING AN EYE OUT

Tommy returned to work, and we were back on the day shift. The temperature was in the nineties, and the radio car had no air conditioner. We were soaked in sweat, and our uniform shirts and leather gun belts oozed perspiration. The last thing we wanted to do was get involved in a brawl. It was not to be.

We got a call to go to Third Avenue and twenty-eighth Street, to investigate a fight in the street. When we got half a block away I recognized Tony Argenziano, the manager of the Gristede's grocery store. He and a junkie were punching away at each other in the middle of Third Avenue. Taking one look at Tony's opponent, it was obvious that he caught a thief as he left the store. Even though it was hot as Hades, the junkie had on a shoplifter's overcoat, with numerous inside pockets to hide the stolen goods.

Every time the shoplifter threw a punch, another item of swag would fall from his coat, onto the street – smoked oysters, crab meat, steaks and salmon. This guy only stole the good stuff. Just as we approached the battling duo, the store manager hauled off and hit the thief with a tremendous right cross, right below his left eye. It was such a hard blow that it knocked the junkie's glass eye right out of the socket. As we got out of the radio car the junkie was on his knees desperately trying to find his eye that was now rolling around on the Third Avenue pavement.

The onlookers screamed because they could now see into the thief's head through the empty eye socket. After retrieving his glass eye, the junkie couldn't put it back in the socket. All the store manager wanted was the stolen merchandise back, and he told the thief not to come in the store any more.

The junkie, now very pissed off because his eye had been knocked from his head, said out loud to Tony "I'm going to get a gun and come back here and kill you."

Without missing a beat McInerney said "Well, pal, you better keep an eye out for the police."

The onlookers roared with laughter, and the tense situation was somewhat diffused for the moment. The battlers went their separate ways. One person in the crowd failed to see the humor in Tommy's quip. She was a pompous, tight-ass, humorless, public school teacher, who practically ran the seven blocks to the station house to make a civilian complaint .... for insensitivity to the handicapped.

The irate woman bolted into the 13th Precinct and began to tell her story to Lt. Von Richter. She went on and on in detail about the junkie and the store manager fighting on Third Avenue. When she got to the part about the glass eye popping out and rolling around on the street", Otto was trying hard not to laugh in the woman's face.

A Police Officer named Bobby Bodenschatz was standing next to the desk, listening to the whole story. As she got to the part where McInerney said to the junkie "You better keep an eye out for the police", Von Richter and Bodenschatz both lost it, and could not stop laughing for a few minutes.

When Bodenschatz recovered, he told the complainant "Lady, a man could wait his whole lifetime for a line like that."

Incensed, the bitch flew out of the Precinct without making her complaint.

MUMMY DEAREST

Driving along East 14th Street in front of Stuyvesant Town, two elderly women flagged us down. They were residents of Stuy Town and they used to attend daily mass with another woman, Doreen Donegan, whom they haven't seen in several months.

Mrs. Donegan lived at 6 Stuyvesant Oval on the 10th floor, with her adult son, Edward. The ladies told us that the son always seemed very strange. Lately, whenever they knocked on the door, Edward was always evasive when asked about his mother. The ladies grew suspicious, and decided to contact the police.

After notifying the dispatcher of our 'pick-up' job at Stuyvesant Town, we proceeded to the tenth floor of Stuyvesant Oval. After knocking on the door, Edward, the woman's son, looked through the peep-hole to see who it was. We announced ourselves as police officers, but he could not see us. Veteran cops know enough not to stand directly in front of a door, otherwise you could be hit by gunfire coming from inside the apartment if some nut inside opens up on you with a gun. We found ourselves in a Mexican standoff with the tenant. We kept knocking on the door, and, after some cajoling, he finally opened up. The air coming out of the small apartment had a musty, fetid odor to it. It was obvious that Edward was somewhat of a mental case. The man looked disheveled and hadn't shaved for weeks. And, there was this eerie look in his eyes, looking like a character in a horror movie. He let us in and told us that his mother was sleeping on the couch.

I had the beejeesus scared out of me as we came into the living room and saw the corpse of the mother lying on the couch. She

103

had been dead for a long time, maybe three months, with fresh flowers strewn all over her body. This was a new one for me. The mother's decomposed body had a gray, leathery consistency to it, unlike anything Tommy or I had ever seen.

The son had masked the smell with flowers and Lysol. He was so nuts that he really didn't know that his mother was dead. His anal retentive personality did not allow flies in the apartment, so there were no maggots to attack the body.

Sgt. Byrne came to the scene. We did a thorough search for valuables, cash, and the decedent's will, and took everything for safekeeping. Edward was taken to Bellevue Psycho for a much needed check-up from the neck-up. The boss said no criminal charges should be brought against the son, since he was obviously not mentally competent. All they could get on him anyway was a petty charge under the Health Code, for failing to promptly report a death. By the time we finished the paperwork, it was 4:45 P.M., and it was off to the Anawanda for a cold one or two. When Tommy and I came in, there was Victor Velez sitting at the bar in his shorts. We quickly realized that it was payday, and ran back to the station house to get our checks, which Mr. McSorley promptly cashed for us.

Back at the bar we met Sky King and The Admiral and told our tale of the mummified mommy. They, in turn, told their story of going to 75 5th Avenue, where they met some rich eccentric who had wallpapered his entire apartment with aluminum foil, and was wearing a tinfoil hat. The man told them that he was repelling the invisible, cancer causing rays sent by his neighbors. They had obviously met Mr. Tunnington.

I said out loud to everyone "Well, boys, we may not be making a lot of money, but we sure as hell have a front row seat to the greatest show in the world."

CUCCARACHA, CUCCARACHA

There was no mistaking the hue and cry coming from a group of angry citizens chasing a burglar down the block. He was caught breaking into an apartment on Lexington Avenue and high-tailed it out of there with the posse right behind him. The thief ducked into the Elton Hotel, the scene of the tear gas fiasco a few weeks earlier. I recognized the same rodent-faced desk clerk, whom I had named "Rat Boy."

Rat Boy quickly gave up the burglar and advised that he sometimes crashed in an empty room on the sixth floor. There were about half a dozen empty rooms on the sixth floor, and the lighting capacity in the filthy, stinking hallway was about ten watts. As we entered the third room, I could not find the light switch. It was pitch black inside. Wherever we walked, a distinctive crackling noise was heard.

I said "Tommy, some asshole put peanut shells all over the floor."

Just then, McInerney found the switch, and turned on the light.

He shouted out "Holy shit, Jimmy! Those aren't peanut shells, they're fucking cockroaches – thousands of them."

The floor, walls, and ceiling were black with roaches. They were all over our uniforms, and were crawling up our legs. All I could say was "What the fuck, Tommy! What the fuck!"

We bolted down the stairs like mad men, and stopped in the lobby. Rat Boy was hysterical, watching us do the Irish jig trying to get the roaches off of us. Upon further questioning the desk clerk came up with a name, and this one was going to be solved by the detectives.

Arriving at the station house, scratching all the way, we told Lt. von Richter what happened. He told us to take all of out clothes off in the shower stall, in case there were any 'stragglers.' Otto was right on the money, because we found roaches in our socks, underwear and butt cracks. Even after showering and changing clothes, we spent the rest of the tour scratching all over.

ET TU, BRUTE!

Police Officer Angelo Terranova was an old time 13th Precinct cop. He was a forty year old bachelor from Bath Beach, Brooklyn. Angelo had no regular partner, and did the odd jobs in the station house, like switchboard operator, security, cell attendant, and filling in for vacations. At seven-fifteen in the morning, Terranova came into the front door of the Precinct, smoking a huge cigar, wearing tan Bermuda shorts, and a sleeveless, white T-shirt that cops call a *wife beater shirt.*

As soon as Lt. Cantorwicz spotted him, he yelled out from behind the desk "Hey, Ang' you look just like a Brooklyn guinea."

"Right, Loo, that's because I am a Brooklyn guinea. At least I was up until last week. While I was on vacation, I bought a house in Staten Island, just over the bridge."

"Well, congratufuckinglations, Ang!" replied Uncle Carl.

But, Angelo was not happy with his new neighborhood. He told the boss "I love the house, Loo, but with my bad luck, I have this *geep* living next door to me. He has a dog that is bigger than a goddam Great Dane. I don't know what it is, but it comes out of this greaseball's house twice a day and leaves a mound of crap on my front lawn about eight fucking inches high. I tried talking to the guy, and all he says is "It ain't-a my-a dog-a. Leave-a me alone-a."

"The other day I caught the dog right in the act, knocked on the guy's front door, and got right in his face over it. He told me that he knows I'm a cop and he'll make a complaint that I pulled my gun out on him, so I'll get fired. I just don't know what the hell to do."

Overhearing the story was P.O. Sean Dennihy, the former Highway Patrol cop. He was paired off with Angelo that day for the first time. Having heard the story of the crapping canine, Dennihy sympathized with Terranova. A cop is always vulnerable to these types of phony complaints.

Angelo was not in defeatist mode, however. He had to figure out a way to get back at this wise-ass immigrant, without the *gavone* knowing that it was him. His assignment this day was to patrol Madison Square Park and the surrounding area, and harass the drug dealers who set up shop there. Dennihy had patrolled the area many times over the summer, and was a pretty sharp cop. He studied the habits of the drug dealers, and knew the major players. To avoid getting caught with felony weight drugs the dealers hid their stash near them, usually in paper bags that looked like discarded trash.

The cops got wise and started sweeping the park, looking into every paper bag, knapsack and container left lying around. This day was no exception, and Sean and Angelo found a treasure trove of pills, marijuana and heroin. While having coffee, Dennihy told his partner that his brother-in-law, O'Toole, a Nassau County cop, had a similar problem with his neighbor. The issue was resolved nicely; well, nicely for O'Toole, but not so nicely for the dog.

Angelo listened attentively to Dennihy's story, and it gave him a great idea. They did not voucher the majority of the drugs that they found. Angelo held back about 200 pills of various types and about two dozen glassine envelopes of cocaine and heroin. He took them home and dumped everything into an aluminum garbage can, using a baseball bat as a grinder. It looked like a giant mortar and pestle. After ten minutes the pills were ground into a fine powder, along with the cocaine and heroin. Angelo took the precaution of parking a few blocks away and walked to his house, so his neighbor would think he was not at home. Usually, the *geep* left the dog out for the second time about 10:30 P.M.

Ang' stopped by his old neighborhood in Brooklyn on the way

home and bought three pounds of chop meat. He put the meat in the garbage can and kneaded it into a lethal mélange with the drugs. Like clockwork, the dog came out of the neighbor's house, right on time, and laid a beauty on Terranova's lawn. He saw the whole thing while hiding alongside the other side of his house, so the neighbor couldn't see him.

By this time the garbage can and bat had been surgically scrubbed and rinsed with Clorox, to remove any trace of meat or drugs. Ang' called the dog over and offered him a large plate of chop meat.

The dog devoured the food, like any 150 pound animal would. With that, Terranova took the plate and vaulted over the back fence, onto his rear neighbor's yard. He then walked to his car. The plate was thrown in a dumpster in the next town. Then Angelo went to a neighborhood bar, so he would have a good alibi. Of course, he had purchased a ticket for the 9:30 P.M. movie at the Lane Theater, and kept the stub.

After finishing his last supper, Brutus, the dog, started trotting back to his master's house. About five feet from the owner's door, the dog rolled over on his back, with its four feet in the air, and instantly expired in the "dying cockroach" position. When Brutus failed to come back, the owner opened his door and found his beloved animal. The dog was stiff as a board, as if instant rigor mortis had set in.

The *geep* was not just irate, he was insane with rage. He immediately began pounding on Terranova's door and gave up after ten minutes. The local police were called and the neighbor told the cops that Angelo killed his dog. He could offer no proof, and since Ang' was not home, they closed the case out.

Terranova came home around midnight and was immediately accosted by his neighbor. He was a madman, yelling, screaming, and cursing "You kill-a my-a dog-a, you sunnamabeetch-a; sunnamabeetch-a!!! You fuck-in-a basta!"

Angelo played dumb "What the fuck are you so excited about,

109

Guido. It ain't-a your-a dog-a. Remember? Go fuck-a youself, you guinea bastard!"

He knew enough to keep his mouth shut forever. And the neighbor's new dog was kept locked in his back yard from now on.

"NO WINE, MESSIEURS?"

Terry Malloy was now a free man. After sending the hated cavalier to his doom, and his wife to divorce court, he began to hang around with Vinny "Sabu" Quaranta. Sabu was dating a girl from Brooklyn, named Connie, and she had a friend, Theresa, who wanted to meet Terry. They planned a double date after the 8 x 4 shift on a Wednesday night. The girls were straight out of Central Casting for the role of "Brooklyn Guidette." At about 4:30 P.M., they met up in front of the Precinct. Sabu was resplendent in his iridescent green leisure suit; Malloy wore a black jacket and tan slacks.

Connie and Theresa wanted to go to a fancy French Restaurant named La Bonne Auberge on East 44th Street. Sparing no expense, the boys sprang for the $3.50, twenty three block cab ride. The interior of the restaurant was beautiful, but the pretentious, snooty waiter, Maurice, turned off Vinny and Terry immediately. Both men were military veterans and were just glad to eat a meal without waiting on line first. The ambiance of the place was lost on them.

Connie, no intellectual, was telling the story of the homeless man she saw the day before, who was so skinny and malnourished that he looked *emancipated*.

The dignified Maurice, a tall, slim man in his late fifties, came to the table for the drink order. He had a pencil thin gray mustache, long sideburns, and thinning salt and pepper hair combed to the side. The girls wanted Bacardi cocktails, Terry ordered beer, and Vinny asked for a Chivas Regal on the rocks.

Maurice pulled up his lanky 6'3" frame and stood there, appalled, saying "No wine, Messieurs?"

Vinny, not pleased with his arrogant attitude, said "I doooon't think soooo, *muss-you-hah*!"

Maurice then got this look on his face like he was sniffing shit, turned on his heels, and left in a huff.

Choosing dinner in this place was quite a task for these four working class people. They all liked soup, so when Maurice returned to take the order, Terry said "Hey, Moe, we'll have four bowls of the *vicky-choize* soup."

Maurice was outraged that the word *vichyssoise* was so fractured. He said in his most haughty French accent "Monsieur, do you mean zhat you are ordering zuh vichyssoise?"

"Yeah, that's it. Bring it right out, Moe, four of them."

Ten minutes later, Maurice brought the soup to the table. As soon as Vinny tasted it he said "Hey, Moe, this soup is cold. Take it back and heat it up."

Maurice's patience was wearing thin, and he said "Monsieur, vichyssoise is a zoop zhat is supposed to be served cold."

Vinny, now on his third drink, and pissed off that he was being lectured to by the waiter, said "Look, Froggy, I don't give a shit what you think. Take this fucking soup back and heat it up."

Maurice was now steaming, and in high dudgeon. "This is a five star restaurant, with the best chefs in New York City. We don't lower our standards for *anyone, of any class,* in society. And my name is Maurice, not Froggy, not Moe."

That was enough for Vinny. "You're a phony Frenchman! I'll bet that your real name is Morris, and you live in the Bronx."

That was enough for Maurice, and the four of them were kicked out, after paying for the drinks and the soup. Anyway, Sabu was half right: Morris lived in Kew Gardens, Queens.

Terry had a good idea, since all four of them were starving. "Let's go to the Anawanda Club. At least we can get some American food that we can identify."

At E. 44th Street and Second Avenue, the two couples piled into a cab and were quickly at E. 20th Street. Once inside, they

112

ordered hamburgers, fries and more drinks. They were having such a good time that they proceeded to get sloshed. When they finished eating, Vinny announced "Let's go swimming in my pool."

The girls felt that he was kidding, until Terry said "We have an indoor pool next door; come on, we'll show it to you."

Within minutes, the four of them were balls-ass naked in the Police Academy pool, having a blast. Soon after that, the two couples were paired off in the shallow end of the pool, assuming the lip-lock, grab-ass position. Terry had not dipped his wick in a long time, and he took Theresa into a dark corner and laid her down on the exercise mats. Unknown to Terry, Theresa hadn't been porked in well over two years. She had slimmed down to 120 pounds after her husband left her for another woman. She looked great now, especially in the dim light. Her cottage cheese ass was well hidden.

They started playing *hide the sausage*. Terry had barely mounted her when he thought he was riding a bucking bronco. After resting a few minutes, they were ready for Act Two.

Connie and Vinny were at the other end of the pool. Connie was a sexual animal. She soon had Sabu on his back, and was riding him like a jackhammer. Vinny thought that it wasn't so bad after all, losing his vice detail and being back on patrol again.

"...THERE'S NOTHING
WE CAN DO."

It was a busy Friday night, when we got a call to the fourth floor of 439 2nd Avenue, report of "difficulty breathing." Traffic was light, and we were there quickly. With no elevator in the building, we ran up the stairs, and on the fourth floor we were met by a sobbing couple in their forties.

We were let into the neat, middle class apartment, and there on the floor lay a twelve year old boy, dead as the proverbial doornail. His name was Louis and he had Down Syndrome. The kid was extremely overweight. The boy's face was blue, and his body was cold. The only thing we could do was to wait for the ambulance to come to officially pronounce Louis dead. He had no pulse, and it appeared that he died of a massive heart attack.

The family was screaming hysterically and demanded that we do something to bring their child back to life. CPR was out of the question; the boy was cold to the touch. I told the family "He's been gone too long. I'm very sorry, but there is nothing we can do."

I felt like such a cold hearted bastard, but I had to tell them the truth.

Everyone started crying. All Tommy and I could do was to cry along with them. This was a close-knit, loving, Italian family, and the deceased's parents, maternal grandparents, and brother and sister were in the apartment. I had an idea to call the local church, and Father Langella from St. Stephen's came right over. He was a great comfort to the family, and it took some heat off of us. The Assistant Medical Examiner arrived promptly, since his office was only a couple of blocks away.

The M.E. was very professional, yet sympathetic to the family's loss. He went over Louis' medical history and learned that the boy was being treated for heart disease at the N.Y.U. Medical Center. The cause of death was heart attack. Once the M.E. closed the case, the local funeral parlor was notified, and our job was done.

I just felt so damn useless. Here we were—cops—hired to help people, and all we could do was just stand there, crying like two blubbering fools. "Damn! This job can be depressing at times", I thought.

Although I saw dozens of dead people before, and many since, the specter of seeing that young boy lying lifeless on the floor would haunt me forever.

The death of a child, even to the outsider, is a gut-wrenching experience, and the pain to the parents and grandparents is unimaginable. To myself, I quietly questioned the existence of God. Tommy and I never spoke of this case ever again.

CANDYGRAM FOR MRS. BRYSON

The phone rang one night around eleven o'clock. It was a friend of the family, Jerry Callahan. Jerry was our lawyer, and he loved his scotch. One good thing about being an honest cop is that if your phone rings late at night, you know it's just one of your friends with his load on, and not a prosecutor or some boss from Internal Affairs.

Callahan was stewed to the gills, and very despondent. We had met in a local tavern two weeks earlier and he knew I was on the balls of my ass, financially speaking.

"Jimmy, I need your help on one of my cases. I am trying to have a will admitted in the Richmond County Surrogate's Court. One of the decedent's heirs has to be served with a Citation and a copy of the will. She didn't receive anything in the will, so she's being a real bitch about it and won't open the door for the process server. I need personal service on her or I'll have to do the work all over again. I have a big fee riding on this one, Jimmy, and I really need it. Can you help me out?"

"What do I have to do, Jerry?"

"Look, Jimmy, you're an experienced cop, and you know how criminals and smart-asses think. How can I get this broad to open the fucking door and serve her with the goddamn papers? She's being a total cunt about it."

"Well, Jerry, all women like getting gifts of flowers and candy. I have an empty cookie tin and I can put rocks in it, then get some balloons and attach them. Most women will open the door for that kind of delivery."

"Good. I'll pick you up at your house at 7:00 P.M. tomorrow."

The next evening, Callahan showed up with a buzz on, driving his fire engine red, '67 Coupe de Ville convertible, and reeking of Dewars. He drove us to a dark, quiet, tree lined street on the north shore of Staten Island with a neat row of one family homes. Seeing the lights on in the red shingled high ranch, Jerry drove around the corner to Victory Boulevard and called the subject, Ann Bryson, from a pay phone.

"Mrs. Bryson?"

"Yes. Who is this."

"This is Tony, the dispatcher from Willowbrook Florists. We tried to make a delivery earlier, but nobody was home. Can my boy come over now?"

"Yes, we'll be home all night."

"Oh, just one thing, Mrs. Bryson, the delivery boy is the boss' nephew and he's a little slow mentally, if you catch my drift. So please don't be mean to him."

"Of course not."

Callahan slowly pulled his big Caddy up to the house, then parked about three houses away, to avoid detection. I got out of the car and walked up the sidewalk with the cookie tin and balloons in my left hand, and the Citation and copy of the will in my right hand. Upon ringing the bell, the subject's husband answered the door. Mr. Bryson was a giant of a man, well over 300 pounds, and sported a black Van Dyke beard. He wore faded jean shorts and a food stained wife-beater shirt.

I could tell that this man was not into stand-up comedy, and I quickly realized that I was in very serious trouble. The large scar on his face indicated that the guy was a brawler. This scenario was certainly not in Coach Callahan's game plan, and I began to feel very, very alone, and totally butt-fucked beyond belief. Whatever money I was getting for this service of process was not enough.

The man made a grab for the cookie tin. I tried to play dumb and said "No, mister. My boss said I have to give this to Mrs. Bryson."

Just then, the intended recipient appeared at the doorway and brushed her husband aside. "It's all right, son. I'll take it from you."

As soon as I finished giving her the balloons and cookie tin, I said "I also have this for you, ma'am," as I handed her the Citation and copy of the will. I strode down the walk, nice and easy, until I heard the pounding footsteps and the bellowing voice of a very pissed off Mr. Bryson right behind me.

He was screaming "WHAT THE FUCK IS THIS? COME BACK HERE, YOU SLIMY LITTLE COCKSUCKER! I'LL FUCKING KILL YOU!

I knew a threat when I heard one, and high-tailed it to Jerry's Coupe DeVille, with one highly agitated giant gaining on me. I ran for my life, dove into the Caddy and screamed "Get the fuck out of here now, Jerry!"

Callahan put the big convertible in gear and peeled out, just as Bryson was banging on the trunk of the car. Luckily, our adversary could not run more than half a block, or he could have killed us both. Jerry was laughing so hard that he could not drive any longer, and pulled over three blocks away. It took several minutes for the both of us to regain our composure.

Callahan whipped out an Affidavit of Service for me to sign and gave me a crisp, new $100 bill. As I was being dropped off at home, Jerry said "Jimmy, did I tell you that guy Bryson just got out of jail for manslaughter? He beat a guy to death in a bar for looking at him funny."

"No, you fucking didn't, Jerry. I almost get killed by this big motherfucker, and *now* you tell me he's a homicidal maniac? Well, thank you very much, *Clarence Fucking Darrow*!.

My gut feeling told me that this was not the last job I would do for Gerald B. Callahan, Esq., although I wished it were.

"AS A DETECTIVE, ZARULLO IS USELESS AS... "

It was 12:45 A.M. and the 4 x 12 shift was in high gear at the Anawanda Club.

Detective Freddie Zarullo, for all of his failings, was one of the most well-like cops in the 13th Precinct. Whenever Freddie held court in the bar there was always a huge crowd around him, listening to his funny, bullshit war stories. As one wag quipped, "Freddie had a great future behind him."

Zarullo was bemoaning the fact that he had to actually leave the station house that day to investigate a homicide in Union Square Park. He let it be known that he was looking for a marijuana dealer in his early 20's, a guy named "Andy." The suspect cut the throat of a rival drug dealer in front of fifty witnesses, forty-seven of whom said they saw nothing. Freddie had nothing else to go on.

Listening to the story, I immediately knew the man he was talking about. "Freddie, is he a flashy dresser, *swordsman* type, with slick black hair, and a gold medallion chain around his neck?"

Freddie damn near popped a woody on the spot. "Yeah, that's the guy."

I told him "The man's name is Arbuto Rodriguez, and he lives on the F.D.R. Drive in the 9th Precinct. We locked him up about two weeks ago. He's a major grass dealer in Union Square Park. He comes in the park in the afternoon, after Joe the Jew and Victor Velez make their collars for the day."

Leaving my beer on the bar, I walked around the corner to the Precinct and found my old arrest report. After making a copy, I returned to the bar and gave it to Zarullo. Nothing further was said

119

about it that night.

Freddie had a major blowout with Sgt. Herring the day before regarding his lethargy, and he was hell-bent on making a spectacular arrest to upstage him. He left the bar about 2 A.M. and returned to the Detective Squad room. Instead of going to bed, he called downtown to the Bureau of Criminal Identification, and ordered Arbuto Rodriguez' mug shots. When he woke up at 7:30 A.M., a messenger had already brought the photos to the Precinct.

The first thing that morning, Detective Zarullo had the three witnesses come to the station house to view a photo array of suspects. They all picked out Rodriguez.

Now, armed with three positive I.D.'s, and all of the suspect's personal information, Freddie called Rodriguez at home and told him that his name came up in the investigation of an armed robbery of a social club. Arbuto, knowing that he never did a hold-up, showed up at 1:00.P.M. to proclaim his innocence. Pre-armed with his three witnesses' identifications, and my information, Freddie had his probable cause for an arrest. As soon as Arbuto arrived in the squad room, he was placed under arrest for murder and put in the holding pen. At least, this time, Freddie Zarullo got up from his desk.

The next day the headlines in the New York Daily News read: "GRAMERCY PARK BULLS CRACK MURDER CASE"

On my way in to work that afternoon I bought the newspaper at the St. George side of the ferry terminal. All the way over to Manhattan I kept reading the story and felt that somehow, I must have missed our names. There was no way they could write this story without mentioning Tommy and me. After several readings, I realized that we were not in the article. However, the column did commend Detective Frederick Zarullo of the 13th Precinct Detective Unit in glowing terms for quickly solving the murder case, through "old fashioned detective work."

As soon as I got to work, I ran up the steps to the squad room. Freddie was there with his feet on the desk, sucking on a Lucky

Strike, and blowing smoke rings toward Sgt. Herring's office. He was grinning like the mangy mutt who just screwed the neighbor's pedigree poodle. I showed him the story, which he had already read many times, and said "Freddie, so you solved this case all by yourself, right?"

Zarullo had this sheepish look on his face when he said "Come on, Jimmy. This is the story that the press wants, so I gave it to them. For Christ's sake, I was just jerking them off. You know, with them, it's one big hand-job"

I was incensed. "Freddie, you couldn't even say that two uniformed cops gave you the lead? Well, you know what, from now on, I'm not giving you jack-shit. The only true thing in the story is that you solved the case through old fashioned detective work – by drinking in a bar." Sergeant Herring also read the story of Zarullo making the big homicide collar. He asked Detective Joe Hughes what really happened, knowing that Freddie could not have done this on his own. Hughes, not wanting to be the rat, tap danced a bit, then, under pressure, told the boss that a uniformed cop gave Zarullo the suspect's name, address, apartment number, date of birth, and telephone number. The cop even gave Freddie a copy of the guy's prior arrest report at the Anawanda Club bar. All Zarullo did was call the suspect to come to the squad room. As soon as he arrived, he got collared for homicide.

To top it off, Captain Hennessey from the Manhattan South Detectives called Sergeant Herring to congratulate him and Zarullo on the good arrest in the Union Square homicide. "Hey, Sarge, that guy Zarullo is one great detective. Gets a burglar last week, and a murder collar this week. Maybe it's time to put Freddie in for Second Grade Detective."

It would have been a better move to grab a Brahma bull by the balls and twist, than to say that to Sgt. Herring.

Steaming, he replied to Captain Hennessey: "Cap', with all due respect, the only reason Freddie Zarullo is a fucking third grade detective is because they don't make fourth grade. A uniformed cop gave him everything but the suspect's circumcision status. He made one mother-fucking phone call to the perp's house, and the jerk came in and surrendered. On his own, this schmuck couldn't find his own ass in a shithouse stall. As a detective, fucking Zarullo is useless as tits on a nun. Second grade for this asshole? My Teutonic ass!"

THE SCHNAUZER
MEETS THE NERD

Joseph Morgan Hughes was a second grade detective, and a great investigator. He was a slightly built man, about 45, with prematurely gray hair. His bushy eyebrows, gray beard and mustache gave him the look of a Schnauzer. That became his nickname in the NYPD. Hughes was the exact opposite of Zarullo. Whenever he caught a case, he aggressively investigated it.

Police Officer Arnold Levine had been in the Police Laboratory until June 30th, when he, along with thousands of other cops, was sent back to patrol. Actually, you couldn't say that Arnold went back to patrol, because he had never been there. He had a degree in chemistry, and went right from the Police Academy to the Lab in 1962.

Arnold Levine loved the NYPD. He had also earned a Master's degree in Criminalistics. He wore glasses and looked like a nerd. You would never make him for a cop. Levine had managed to annoy a succession of bosses at the Lab, which is why a man with his qualifications was never promoted to detective.

Working with Arnold was like training a rookie. He had to be taught the most basic things, like using the radio, and not standing directly in front of a door when you knock, in case the person inside starts shooting through the door; and not to hold the flashlight in front of you, but to the side. Levine even had to be taught how to drink coffee like a cop, by peeling back a small part of the cover. In case you get a call, you can seal up the top and drink it later.

Arnold was teamed up with Wayne Harrison, a deeply religious black man from Queens. Wayne was an Evangelical Protestant who had a habit of preaching to prisoners, telling them they would go to hell if they didn't repent. Levine had not been in a synagogue since his uncle Marvin died years ago. They were truly the "odd couple."

Harrison and Levine worked sectors 13 Charlie-David. They were having coffee on a side street when the dispatcher's alert button sounded "In the 13th Precinct, a robbery in progress, 3rd Avenue and East 25th Street, in the supermarket."

Wayne picked up the radio and said "13 Charlie-David responding."

The dispatcher continued "Further information, Charlie, use caution, suspects are three male blacks, all armed."

Arnold reached for the siren, but was instructed by Harrison that on a call like this you don't use the siren, only the roof lights. If you need to move traffic, use the horn. The siren will alert the robbers, who may panic and kill the victims, or they may be waiting to cut you down when you show up.

Wayne was a street-smart cop, and knew enough not to pull up directly in front of the store. He parked on the side of the building and walked up to the store, not on the sidewalk, but on the street. That way, in case their boys came out smoking, they could take cover behind a car. They were met by an employee of the store who informed them that the suspects fled north on 3rd Avenue in a green Chevy Nova.

Inside, the store manager lay on the floor, shot in the abdomen. Levine, never having seen a shooting victim before, started to get queasy when he saw the crimson pool of blood spilling out onto the white tile floor. His partner sensed this and gave Arnold something to do: "Go get some towels so I can try to stop the bleeding."

The victim had lost a lot of blood, and the ambulance arrived quickly from Bellevue Hospital. Wayne called the Detective Squad. Luckily, Detective Joe Hughes was on duty. The Schnauzer came right to the scene and began questioning witnesses. Hughes had a knack for interviewing people to get the most information from them. There were four employees who said that they could positively identify the suspects. They were taken in to the squad room to view mug shots.

Before leaving, Hughes asked the witnesses if they had seen any of the robbers touch anything. A clerk informed him that the shooter picked up a cardboard box filled with cans of vegetables and threw it at the manager, just prior to shooting him. The Detective was disappointed because he thought that it was impossible to get fingerprints from cardboard. Levine was privy to the conversation and heard Hughes' theory about not being able to retrieve prints from cardboard. Arnold said "Detective Hughes, that's not true. You can get prints from cardboard, by using Ninhydrin."

"You're shitting me. What the hell is that stuff? I never heard of it," said the skeptical detective.

"Well, you have to use the Ninhydrin solution so that it brings out the fingerprints on the irregular cardboard surface. If there are any latent prints, they will come out in a purple color. I used to work in the Lab, and I know how to do it."

With that, Arnold went to the radio car and took out his fingerprint kit. In a few minutes, he had developed ten perfect fingerprints. Hughes was impressed.

The prints were sent by messenger to the Bureau of Criminal Identification (BCI). Within less than an hour, they got a hit. The shooter was Jonathan Mosely from Walton Avenue in the Bronx. He was a violent career criminal who was wanted for several other robberies. His accomplices were also identified by the witnesses.

About an hour later Bellevue Hospital called the 13th Detective Squad and notified Detective Zarullo that the store manager had died. Freddie, tactless as always, yelled across the squad room "Hey, Schnauz', Bellevue called. Your store manager just cashed in his chips."

This time, thought Hughes, Mosely will be put away forever. Joe Hughes obtained an arrest warrant for the three suspects for Murder 2 and Robbery 1. The first order of priority was to lock up the shooter, Mosely. Sergeant Herring, Hughes and Zarullo were the only detectives working. Sgt. Herring was not happy about having to make a collar up in the Bronx with Freddie along, but he was the only act in town. As a courtesy to the local Precinct, they called the 42nd Pct. Detective Squad and asked for a back up at a tenement on Walton Avenue.

Upon arrival at the apartment building, they were met by 42 Squad Detectives, Romeo Santiago and Guadalupe "Lupe" Rios-Rivera. Sgt. Herring, Hughes and Rios-Rivera went up to apartment 4D. The Sergeant directed Zarullo and Santiago to guard the alley in case the suspect fled via the fire escape.

At the fourth floor apartment, they walked through the hallway of dirty, puke-colored paint, with roach corpses strewn on the floor, belly up. The Schnauzer knocked at the door, and shouted "Police, open the door."

Inside the apartment, a squeaky female voice said "Who dat?"

Hughes, getting visibly pissed off, said "It's the police; open the door."

Again, from inside the same voice said "Who dat?"

This time, Detective First Grade Lupe Rios-Rivera, a long time ghetto cop, brushed Hughes aside and said "It's the **POH**- LEECE, **OPEN** the goddam door, lady."

The voice inside replied "Well, whyn't you say so da foist time?"

Jonathan's mother opened the door half way, revealing a black woman in her mid-forties, with a head of salt and pepper hair, who looked washed out. She had probably lost twenty years off her life due to her worthless son.

Detective Hughes showed her the arrest warrant and said "Where's Jonathan? We have an arrest warrant for him. Is he here?"

I ain't seen him for a few days, officuh."

The experienced Detectives could tell she was lying to protect her son.

Just then, the detectives heard a noise in the bedroom. It was Jonathan, making his escape out the bedroom window. He was

126

down the fire escape in seconds.

Detective Santiago was stationed at one end of the long alley, and Freddie Zarullo was at the other end, hiding behind a large green dumpster. Mosely dropped the last four feet from the fire escape ladder, and bolted toward the dumpster.

Freddie, not one to unnecessarily burn off any calories, waited until the suspect came closer, then stuck out his foot and tripped Mosely, sending him head first into a brick wall. While he was unconscious for a few seconds, Freddie was on top of him, rear cuffed the prisoner, and had the dazed Mosely face-down on the concrete slab.

Herring, Hughes and Rios raced down the stairs to assist, only to find Freddie standing next to the robbery suspect, with fedora askew, and smoking a Lucky Strike. He had his left foot on the perp's back, posing like some big game hunter in Africa who had just bagged his trophy. If looks could kill, Herring's would have killed Zarullo on the spot. Not a word was spoken in the car all the way downtown. This time, Sgt. Herring saw to it that Levine and Harrison received the proper departmental recognition that they deserved. The Schnauzer took the collar.

MARGIE FOGARTY BLABS

Margie Fogarty, the civilian employee from the Police Academy, did a lot of voice-overs for the NYPD training films. She was also the woman who conned Sgt. Sven Nordstrom into appearing for his audition as a U.S.M.C. Drill Sergeant. Margie maintained complete silence since early July. One major problem was that she liked her sauce; scotch and water to be precise, and she liked it a lot.

In early August, Margie and her friends stopped at the Anawanda Club after work. After a few drinks, Fogarty started up about the Nordstrom incident. The NYPD has its gossips and rumormongers, and they were all listening to her story. Everyone in the 13th Precinct and the Police Academy knew what happened to Sgt. Nordstrom, but nobody knew who the players were behind it. It was, until now, a well-kept secret.

Thankfully, Margie did not name anyone, but Nordstrom soon found out from his spies who the person was who set him up for his public humiliation. He confronted Margie Fogarty at her job and began to badger her to give up the name of the 13th Pct. cop who was behind the scheme. When Nordstrom got nasty and started to threaten her, Margie went into her boss, Lt. Jensen, and told him what was happening. Jensen pulled rank, kicked Nordstrom out of the office, and told him to stay out.

Nordstrom was like the modern day Captain Ahab, searching for his Great White Tormentor. He was nearly insane, trying to figure out who did it to him.

He initially suspected Dennihy, Quaranta and Podolsky, but

128

had no proof. Nordstrom was desperately trying to recall the day that Daphne Young came into the Precinct. Who was there at the time? Who was near the desk? Who, Who, who?

The switchboard operator on that shift was Darlene Pignatano. Nordstrom's opinion of her was that she was a scatterbrained bimbo from Bath Beach, and mentally incapable of pulling off a stunt like the one pulled on him. Looking at the roll call, he realized that Darlene had gone to lunch, and had to be relieved by a Police Officer. Who the hell was it?

The day shift roll call had my name as a hand written entry, meaning I had made an arrest the previous night, and was going to court in the morning. Nordstrom checked the blotter and saw that Lt. Cantorwicz made an entry showing that P.O. Kavanaugh came back from court around noon. As the odd man out, I had to be the switchboard relief. Yes, I, Jimmy Kavanaugh, was beginning to look more and more like a suspect. But Nordstrom was confused, since he had never screwed me over since I got there. I always treated him with respect, and never had a problem with him. He was so paranoid that he even suspected Uncle Carl.

Sgt. Nordstrom began to hang out in the Anawanda, trying to pry information from people who had too much to drink, which classified most of the patrons. The women all knew his reputation and treated him like a loser. Captain Ahab was locked and loaded, and looking to harpoon me as his Moby Dick.

WEST SIDE STORY

Podolsky and Mulligan worked the west side and were a good team. Their sector, 13 Henry-Ida, had been hit with a series of commercial burglaries over the past three weeks. They could not determine who was doing it, but it was the same person, based on the modus operandi. The thief anchored a rope on the roof, then lowered himself down and kicked in a window for entry. It was a very low tech operation.

They did have a suspect, a skinny junkie named Daryl Hayes. The radio car team would stop and frisk him, and always came up with nothing. They Daryl would end the confrontation with his usual "Fuck you, cops!"

Freddie Zarrullo was assigned to investigate all of the recent burglaries. He figured out that the thief would plant the rope on the roof during the day, then come back at night and finish the job. Freddie told Sgt. Herring that he was going over to West 28th and West 29th Streets to search the rooftops for evidence.

Within half an hour he found paydirt – a coiled rope on the roof of 134 West 29th Street, hidden under some debris. Zarullo was a devious, conniving man, always looking for the easy solution to things. He took out his switchblade knife and cut about 7/8's through the rope's mid-section, then coiled it back into its original position.

Two days later Freddie got the Daily News and read the page three story of the burglar who fell six stories into the rear of a West 29th Street building after his rope broke. His fall had been broken by some utility wires, and he was in critical condition at Bellevue

Hospital. Zarullo took the collar and went to Bellevue Hospital to fingerprint the prisoner. Sure enough, it was Daryl Hayes. He was in a body cast from the waist down, and the man was in great pain.

Freddie could not help snickering. "Have a little problem with your rope last night, son?", as he popped his switchblade knife open and kissed it.

"Looks like you're one turkey who can't fly. Have a nice fucking day, scumbag."

Daryl got the point that he had been supremely butt-stroked by the cops. And to top it off, Freddie got to legitimately close out every commercial burglary on the west side for the past year, based on the modus operandi of the suspect.

THANK YOU, JOE GARCIA

I had the great fortune of having been broken in on the job by a great cop in Greenwich Village's Sixth Precinct, by the name of Joe Garcia. Joe was eight years older than me, and we attended the same high school in Staten Island. From the day I arrived in the Sixth, Joe took me under his wing and taught me how to be a good cop. I never met anyone in my entire life, on or off the job, who had more dignity, grace, class, and common sense. Joe was a great mentor and role model to me. I became the cop that I was, mostly because of Joe's counsel and good example.

The West Village was, and is, filled with clueless liberals who have never swung a bat in the real world. Yet, despite their lack of life experience, they were an outspoken group. Garcia knew this, and worked around the problem.

I had become a good student of Joe's. Sadly, in January, 1975, Joe was killed in the line of duty by an armed robber. He and his partner were chasing a robbery suspect into the subway at Broadway and 8th Street. The robber suddenly turned and Joe and the gunman both shot at point blank range, killing each other. Joe death was a hurt from which I would never recover. I could only keep Joe's memory alive by trying to be as good a cop as he was, and Joe was the best there ever was. It was about 9:00 P.M., and at E. 19th Street and 2nd Avenue we were hailed down by a well-dressed woman in her late forties. She was a smart-ass broad, who started complaining about a sleeping bum about thirty feet from the entrance to her luxury apartment building. Most normal people would have just walked right on by, thinking that it was just a drunk sleeping it off. Not the Manhattan liberal, however.

They are superior to everyone else, more educated, extremely social conscious, and most of all, they want people to know that *they care*. If you don't believe it, just ask one.

Sally Reinhardt said to us "How can you just drive by this poor man and not help him? It is obvious that he's not just some drunken derelict to ignore. He's sick and he needs help. You must remember, *drunk is sick*."

Remembering the lessons taught to me by my idol, Joe Garcia, I said to Tommy "Let me deal with this bimbo."

"Yes, ma'am. I didn't realize that the man was sick. I'm sorry, but I only have a high school education and thought that he was just a sleeping wino. You must have a college degree."

She gushed, "Well, yes, I graduated from Colgate University with a Master's Degree in education. I now teach at N.Y.U."

I said to myself "Now there's half the fucking problem. They don't teach common sense in these schools"

Tommy and I woke up the passed-out drunk and picked him up under the arms, all the while stroking Ms. Reinhardt's massive ego with lines like "You must be a very caring, sensitive person to want to help a poor soul like this; You're such a great humanitarian; You really do care about people, professor." It was a world class hand-job, given with a velvet glove and tube of KY jelly.

Sally was lapping up every word of our *blarney*, the Gaelic word for *bullshit*. Then, in the memory of the late, great Joe Garcia, we started walking the bum closer and closer to the entrance door of the professor's apartment building. As we got near her doorman, I said to her "Professor, do you have an extra bed where we can put this man?"

Sally started to panic and began to tap dance. "No, officer, I only have a one bedroom apartment."

"That's O.K.", I said, "We'll just put him on your couch until he gets better. What floor are you on?"

Before we could get any closer to the entrance, Sally blurted out "You're not putting that stinking bum in my apartment!"

133

I knew I had her, and struck back "But, *drunk is sick*, Professor. You said so, yourself. Can't you help someone who's a little down on his luck and sick? Don't you care about him any more? He's a fellow human being............ he has a mother."

With that, Sally turned on her heels, flew into the lobby, raced for the elevator, and disappeared into the night. Tommy, having caught onto my act, yelled out "Hey, Professor, how about bringing a sandwich down for him?"

I chuckled to myself "Thanks, Joe G." She was just another phony liberal exposed for the fraud that they are.

As I explained to my younger partner, "Liberals think that they are far superior to everyone else, because *they care*. They think that caring makes them so much better than others. The fact that they would never do anything to actually help the poor and the homeless is irrelevant. They just want the world to know that they care."

As Joe Garcia used to say "A liberal is a guy who wrings his hands as he watches someone drown, but wouldn't bother to throw them a life preserver."

PAINFUL FLASHBACKS

Police work can grind a man down, mentally, more than physically. I sensed that it is because of the hours of tedium and boredom, interrupted by moments of sheer terror. It is bad for the nervous system. This week in August had been a rough one, and it had taken its toll on us. I could tell that my normally talkative partner had become withdrawn and sullen, and he was smoking more than usual. Also, Tommy had started drinking bourbon old fashioneds after work, instead of the customary draft beers.

The scene of the car crash victims on the FDR Drive who were hit head on would haunt us forever. Three were killed instantly, and the four survivors were found in grotesque positions, with broken limbs, and severe facial disfigurement.

A bum in a rooming house had his testicles ripped off by another derelict, and they lay on the floor of the dingy hotel room, like two huge kidney beans. Tommy accidentally stepped on one, squashing it into the filthy linoleum floor.

A fight in Connolly's Tavern ended when one combatant bit the middle finger off of his opponent, and spit it out on the bar. I was ready to start drinking bourbon, too. But, of all the calls a cop gets, the ones involving child abuse are probably the worst.

I cringed when I heard Central's call to respond to 245 East 25th Street, apartment 2F, to investigate possible child abuse. We were at the run down tenement in no time, and walked up to the second floor. Actually we had to, since there was no elevator. Tommy knocked on the door with his nightstick; there was no response. Either the victim in the apartment was avoiding us, or was too scared to open the door. Or quite possibly, a concerned

135

neighbor called the police.

We knocked on the neighbor's door and were soon informed that the man in 2F was a nasty drunk who regularly beat his wife and children with his fists and a belt. He was from some Central American country, and was an evil, lazy bastard who did not work, choosing to live off of the system, or more precisely, off the backs of New York City's working population.

Going back to apartment 2F, we knocked so hard that the door nearly came off of its hinges. A portly, unshaven Hispanic man, wearing a beer-stained T-shirt, opened the door slightly and growled "Get out of here. Nobody here called you."

Tommy advised him "Sorry pal, I'm not too good at taking orders. We have to come in and look around. There is a complaint of child abuse in this apartment."

After we pushed our way in, we went over to the wife and three kids cowering in the corner of the living room. The wife had two black eyes, and welts on her arms. The children also had wounds on their arms and necks. I asked the mother to expose the kid's backs. When she lifted up their shirts I became enraged, and filled with a primal anger. I saw deep, reddish-purple trauma marks, and open, oozing, infected wounds that were consistent with a belt lashing.

Sure, they tell you that when you become a cop, you have to put all of your personal feelings aside. In reality, they affect you, and, no matter what, you are the product of all of your prior life experiences. You just can't suddenly act like you've had a full frontal lobotomy, just because you became a cop.

Tommy took the wife and children into the bedroom to get some more information from them. I had seen the look on the woman's face before. It was the look of the battered wife: despair, confusion, fear, and helplessness, along with that silent cry for help for someone to come forward and help them.

With Tommy in the bedroom with the wife and kids, I confronted the husband with the evidence of physical abuse that I had seen. The man's only defense was that where he is from, a man can do anything he wants to discipline his wife and children, even beating them with his fists, belt, stick, or anything else.

I got in the man's boozed-up face and said "You're not in goddamn *Guatafuckingmala*, pal, you're in America. You better start acting like an American."

The man had never heard blunt talk like that. He was used to pabulum-puking social worker types who kissed his ass to avoid being called a racist. His Spanish machismo started to percolate, and he screamed at me "Get out of my house, now!"

I replied "Sorry, pal, but if anybody leaves, it's going to be you."

I took an instant dislike to this violent, Third World piece of crap, and started to develop what cops call *the wild eye*. That's where you just lose control and want to destroy the object of your hatred. When I told the man that he was going to be arrested for assault and child abuse, he went berserk and started to choke me.

"Christ", I thought, "I can't let this greasy bastard just choke me to death." I thrust my hands inside his arms, pushed up, and broke the choke hold. My adversary was 5'7" tall, and weighed about 230 pounds. He was built like a 1940 G.E. refrigerator. After I broke free of his grip, he hauled off to hit me in the head with a right cross. I stepped to my left and the punch missed my head, but he hit me in the shoulder so hard that my right arm was paralyzed. I soon realized that I was no match for the guy, so I had one chance with my good hand. He threw another punch at my head and I ducked, then I shot a quick left, straight to his esophagus. The man choked for a moment and I saw my opportunity. I whipped a wicked left hook to his solar plexus, then another, and another. My opponent fell to his knees. He was not beaten yet, and was still dangerous. I knew that if he got up and continued the fight I could not beat him. So I stepped back and kicked him square in the sternum, sending him backwards into the wall. I sprang on him like a tiger, raining left hooks to the right side of his face, never having even thought to call my partner for help.

McInerney heard the commotion and came running out, just

as I began to choke the bum with my one good hand. I had black and white flashbacks of my own violent father and saw him on the floor in front of me, and I wanted to kill the man. My choking took effect right away. The man's eyes were bulging from his head, and he had this weird look on his face like he knew he was going to die. He pissed his pants from sheer fright.

Tommy saw that I had the *wild eye* and yelled "Jimmy, what the fuck are you doing, you're going to kill the fucking guy!", as he struggled to pull me off of him.

Before the ambulance came for the wife and children, I took the father aside and said "Listen up, scumbag. I'm going to come back here every week, and if I see any marks on these kids or your wife, you're going to get a worse beating."

The man gave me a look of utter fear, as well he should have. I still wanted to crush this miserable man like a bug. His wife and children, however, were beaming, having seen their cowardly tormentor rear cuffed and being taken to jail, after getting a well-deserved beating from a cop.

I was in such a blind rage that I didn't realize for the moment that I had sustained a dislocated shoulder. At Bellevue Hospital, Dr. Jennie Chan, all 100 pounds of her, used all of her strength to pop my shoulder back into place, without anesthesia. Most of the pain was gone now. This prisoner was one worthless criminal who I was going to bring to court by myself, pain or no pain. There was no way I was reporting sick.

ELECTROLUX LOVER

While radio runs to Stuyvesant Town were rare, calls to the more exclusive Peter Cooper Village were virtually non-existent. The apartments in Peter Cooper Village were larger, more expensive, and were wired for air conditioning, unlike Stuyvesant Town. The residents were, for the most part, upper middle class, and even wealthy.

The call came in to go to apartment 822, 446 East 23rd Street, and to call the dispatcher from location via land line when we got there. No condition was specified.

Upon arrival at the apartment, we knocked on the door and a voice inside told us to come in. The door was unlocked. Inside the lavishly furnished apartment there was a distinguished looking man in his mid forties, with a bushy black mustache, and thinning black hair, combed straight back. He was sitting on the couch, buck naked. Another minor quirk was that his turgid penis was stuck in the hose of his vacuum cleaner.

This guy was giving himself a blow job with his vacuum and had gotten such a major woody that it wouldn't go down. Tommy called the dispatcher and said

"We have this rich guy in Peter Cooper who was giving himself a knobber with his vacuum cleaner. His dick is stuck in the hose. What the fuck do we do now?"

The dispatcher was an old timer with a sense of humor, and he said "I'll get Emergency Service over there right away. Meanwhile, see if the guy has some nude photos of Bella Abzug. That ought to make him go limp as a dishrag."

Emergency One came to the apartment. Again, it was the team

of Paul Rivetski and Richie Harris. They explained to the man that they have a special saw which can remove the hose without hurting him. He was instructed not to move at all or panic.

About one inch from the top of the guy's dork, Harris gingerly cut the metal tube. Meanwhile, Rivetski was in the kitchen melting butter on the stove. Melted butter is one of the most slippery household substances you can find. Once the butter cooled down Harris poured it into the top of the tube and it slowly worked its way down. With some careful movements, they were able to remove the tube off of the man's penis.

Tommy got the aided person's information. He was Terrence C. Connolly. The name was not familiar to us, nor did we recognize his face. Mr. McSorley, owner of the Anawanda Club, knew nearly everybody in the area. Without giving him any background, he told us that Mr. Connolly was an attorney, and the chief counsel for the local New York State Assemblyman, J. Stewart Lovell. Mr. Lovell was Chairman of the Civil Service Committee and a great supporter of NYPD cops. Mr. Connolly was the power behind the throne in the State Assembly. I put this information in my memory bank, little knowing that it would be of use very soon.

UNION SQUARE SHOWDOWN

As the fates would have it, on August 1st Chief Katzman was replaced as Commanding Officer of Manhattan South by Chief Van Der Steig, late of the Police Academy. Several weeks before, while working at his desk one afternoon, Chief Katzman accidentally poked himself in the eye with his pencil. He then investigated and approved his own line of duty injury, then put himself in for a tax free disability pension, at seventy-five per-cent of his annual salary. He would be known forever into NYPD legend as "Three Quarters Katzman."

Willem Van Der Steig and Dan Fitzgerald were old enemies. In the NYPD there are some small minded men who achieve high rank, and then try to get revenge for every petty grudge and slight they ever experienced on the job. The two men had clashed as Lieutenants in Brooklyn South, some ten years before. Rather than just forgetting it and moving on, Van Der Steig sought to take his revenge out on Captain Fitzgerald by relieving him of his command, and publicly humiliating him.

Chicken-shit, vindictive commanders have an underhanded tactic of sandbagging a subordinate by giving him a task that is doomed to failure, then sacking him for it. Fitzgerald knew that Union Square Park was his Achilles heel. It had become a virtual drug bazaar, with various ethnic groups actually engaging in shooting wars over the most lucrative drug selling locations in the park. The first thing that Chief Van Der Steig did was to give Captain Fitzgerald a direct order to clean up Union Square Park.

It would be difficult, because there were Puerto Ricans, whites, Jamaican Rastafarians and American black drug dealers all vying for the best spots in the park. The Rastafarians were, by far, the most dangerous group in the park. These bastards were just plain crazy. They smoked marijuana joints the size of cigars, drank warm Guinness Stout and cold Heineken beer, thus burning their brain cells out by the millions.

With so many new men now in the command Captain Fitzgerald had to review their personnel files to see if any could take over the job of bring Union Square under control. He found P.O. Victor Velez first. Velez was a good cop, and an experienced investigator from Bronx Narcotics. He was one or two months away from making detective when a Bronx politician had him bounced from Narco on the complaint of a drug dealer, who was a major contributor to the local Councilman's election campaigns.

The C.O. needed one more man with experience, and found the file of P.O. Jack Kalkstein, a former detective from the 90 Pct. in Williamsburg, Brooklyn. Jack had lost his gold shield over a bum rap pushed by an Hasidic rabbi with big time political connections. Kalkstein was a very bitter man who had been screwed over by political hacks. He called himself *Jack the Jew.* Jack had four years to go until retirement.

The Captain had already briefed Sgt. Byrne on the problem, when he called in Velez and Kalkstein. He told the two cops that they had every right to be pissed off at the job, and do nothing as they coasted to their twenty years. But, for the time being, he advised them that he really needed their help for the next few months. They accepted the assignment without hesitation.

Sgt. Byrne would supervise the team for two weeks, then a new Sergeant would take over every two weeks after that, to avoid allegations of being too cozy with the crew. It was idiotic, but that was how the high command in Police Plaza looked at things.

The Captain told them to pick a back-up team for the first week. They chose me and Tommy, and a new crew would be used every week. On the way out of the C.O.'s office, Fitzgerald said "By the way, boys, you will have to work in uniform, on the Chief's

142

orders." This was done to ensure the mission's failure. If you put a bell around the cat's neck, he sure as hell isn't going to catch many mice.

The first day was spent on the rooftops surrounding Union Square Park. High powered binoculars honed in on the major dealers, their locations, and their support staff. Having seen the operation, the team would start tomorrow at 10:00 A.M.

The next day, shortly after 10:00 A.M., Victor and Jack took up a position on the roof of 15 Union Square East. They could see the dealers starting to stake out their positions. The first target was the Rastafarian gang, since they were the major players. The dealers were not stupid, and were clever enough to let some low level moron take the collar for them, without having felony weight seized by the cops. The plan was to catch the higher-ups, and disrupt their daily stash of drugs. Between 10:30 and 10:40 A.M. they observed a red van circling Union Square Park several times. The vehicle was driven by a Rasta, with another riding shotgun. At 14th Street and Union Square East the van pulled up close to the park, and a large duffel bag was brought out, then another. They were handed off to a Rasta, who hid them beneath some shrubbery.

Kalkstein had good instincts as a cop. He got on the radio and told us to stop the red van and hold the occupants. Jack and Victor raced into the park; Velez seized the man who put the duffel bags under the shrubs and recovered felony weight marijuana. Jack then joined me, Tommy and Sgt. Byrne at the red van. Upon opening the back of the van, there was an overpowering stench of marijuana, revealing two more duffel bags of marijuana. Both the driver and the passenger were arrested, as well as their accomplice.

Rastafarians are devious, sneaky, dangerous people, and not to be trusted for even a moment. The men keep their long dreadlocks balled up in a knit hat that looked like a sack on their heads. The street-wise Sergeant Byrne directed us to take their hats off and search their hair. Both the driver and passenger in the van each had a loaded 9 mm pistol hidden in their dirty, greasy dreadlocks.

143

Sgt. Byrne ordered us to bring the evidence and three prisoners into the station house. We had one van, two pistols and 220 pounds (100 kilos) of grass. Not bad for day one. As a precaution, as soon as we got in front of the Precinct, we removed the distributor coil so the van could not start. Jack the Jew knew the Rasta mentality quite well, and he told us we were being watched all the time. On his instructions, we left two duffel bags in the van and waited next door in Emergency One's quarters to see if any Rastas were following us.

Sure enough, a late model silver Dodge van approached the station house. Two Rastafarians jumped out. One tried to start the red van, while the other removed the two duffel bags of drugs and put them in the silver van. Then he came back and opened the back door as if he was looking for something else. With that, Tommy, Sgt. Byrne and I rushed out of ESU's quarters, and in seconds we were on them like flies on shit. They were charged with tampering with evidence, grand larceny (stealing drugs) and felony possession of marijuana. Of course, their brand new vans were seized for forfeiture.

Byrne asked aloud why the man would come back to the vehicle once he already had the drugs. He surmised that there must be something else in the van; it didn't take too long to find out. Lifting up a floor mat, we located the place where the spare tire and jack were stored. Instead of a tire and jack, there was a briefcase loaded with $20 bills. It took us a while, but we counted about $90,000 in cash.

In front of the desk, the head Rasta, Donovan MacKenzie, started into a racial tirade, and accused the cops of preventing him from making an honest living, just because he was black. He blurted out:

"GODDAMN WHITE COPS BREAK MY BALLS!"

Without missing a beat, Lt. Cantorwicz chimed in with a small plastic banjo that he kept behind the desk:

"DOO DAH, DOO DAH"

Then everyone joined in:
"GODDAMN WHITE COPS BREAK MY BALLS,
ALL THE DOO DAH DAY;
THEY STOLE MY DRUGS AND BOTH MY TRUCKS,
DOO DAH, DOO DAH, I GOT NO GRASS, AND NOW I'M
FUCKED,
ALL THE DOO DAH DAY."

The next day would start out the same, with another seizure of the Jamaicans' grass, and the Puerto Ricans and the whites would get collared in the ensuing days. After two weeks the park was pretty quiet, so much so that a normal person could walk through it without being solicited to buy drugs. The dealers didn't disappear, though. They were right under the surface, waiting for the cops to leave, or quietly servicing private clientele in nearby locations.

Captain Fitzgerald, a 26 year veteran, knew the politics of the job. He did not like it, but had to engage in the system in order to survive. His brother-in-law was a reporter for the New York Daily News and the Captain gave him the inside scoop on the clean-up of Union Square Park. Of course, the story did not name any cop's names, or even Fitzgerald's. The article started off by stating that "the master plan of Chief Willem Van Der Steig, the new C.O. of Manhattan South, was a glowing success. The drug dealers had been driven out of Union Square Park."

Most importantly, Chief Van Der Steig's ego had been stroked, and Fitzgerald's job was saved for the time being. The Chief had nothing to do with the success of the mission, but was willing to take credit for it. Captain Fitzgerald knew full well the Eleventh Commandment of the NYPD: "Thou shalt not get more publicity than your superiors, or suffer the consequences."

THE VIKING ZEROES IN

Sgt. Nordstrom continued his Ahab-like quest to find the person who set him up for his supreme humiliation. He narrowed the search down to me and Manny Lopez. Both of us were former Police Academy staff. Manny had no prior working relationship with Margie Fogarty, but Nordstrom found out that I did. Also Tommy and I were in the station house when drill sergeant Nordstrom bolted in.

In the NYPD the walls have ears, and rumors came my way that the Viking suspected that I did him in, and he was gunning for me. Somehow, I had to protect myself from retaliation. Right away, I went upstairs to Manhattan South headquarters. My old Sergeant from the West Village, Ray Munson, was now a Lieutenant, and he was the Personnel Officer for the Borough. The Lieutenant liked me because I had made a lot of good arrests in the Village, and Munson got awarded special assignment money because of some of my collars. I knew that I had to call in a favor from my old boss, or get screwed, big time. Munson had heard of the incident with Sgt. Nordstrom and thought it was funny as hell. I confided in him that I was the one behind it. Thankfully, he responded by saying that it was the best practical joke he had ever heard of in his life. Lt. Munson, my *rabbi*, knew of the Viking's reputation as a bad boss, and he felt that it would be good to get him out of Manhattan South and make him someone else's problem.

Looking through his files, he saw that two years before, Nordstrom had put in for a transfer to Brooklyn South, and apparently forgot about it, after finding out what a great place the 13th was. Munson acted on the old transfer request, and in one phone call, Sgt. Nordstrom was assigned to the 71st Pct. in Brooklyn. On his last day in the 13th Pct. the Viking confronted me in the sitting room. It was just the two of us, all alone.

Nordstrom was an imposing physical specimen. He got right in my face and said "Kavanaugh, you little prick, I know it was you, wasn't it?"

I was in *fight or flight* mode, but there was no way I was fleeing from this encounter, even if I got my ass kicked. Without backing up one inch I got in his face and said "Sarge, you may have rank, but you have no class. It was payback for your humiliation of veteran cops at the roll call. You have no respect for the job, for seniority, or your fellow cops. That's why *your* going away party will be held in a fucking telephone booth on Second Avenue. If you want to make more of it, we can go next door to the gym and put the gloves on. It's your call."

Nordstrom knew that I was a gritty street fighter. He could probably beat me in the ring, with rules, but he would have his good looks ruined while doing so. Using that standard, I had nothing to lose, since I'd been told more than once that I had the perfect face for radio.

He ended the encounter by saying "Fuck you, you Kraut-Mick bastard."

Once Nordstrom was sent packing to the 71, I did not have to buy a drink at the Anawanda for two weeks, having become a mini celebrity in the Precinct.

GERTRUDE, MEIN SCHATZ

Rolf's German-American Restaurant is on the corner of 3rd Avenue and East 22nd Street, right around the corner from the Precinct. Rolf's taps were slightly upgraded from the Anawanda Club's. He had ice-cold Michelob on draft, as well as German beers. My wife and I had been going there for years, long before I was assigned to the Police Academy and the 13th Precinct. The staff remained the same, year after year.

Henry the bartender was a huge hulking man, with blonde hair, mixed with some gray, and he was known as the "gentle giant." That is, until someone gave him a problem. Then, this huge Teutonic titan got his dander up, and threw many a disorderly person through the swinging doors onto 3rd Avenue.

Gertrude "Trude" Schilling was the head waitress. She was a pleasingly plump blonde, in her early fifties, with her weight packed in the right places, if you get my drift. She was all "tits and ass." Trude had a thick German accent. She had known me for many years, because I was a regular in the place. I had been a customer since 1964, the year that Rolf's opened.

After a day tour I went to Rolf's for dinner, along with Tommy, Sabu and The Teen Angel. The three of them had never been there before. Trude greeted me as always: "Guten Abend, mein Freund (Good evening, my friend).

And I answered her with my usual "Guten Abend, mein Schatz. Wie geht es Ihnen?" (Good evening, my treasure, how are you?).

Tommy was introduced as my new partner, and as soon as Trude saw his baby face (he looked about 15 years old) she said "*Chimmy, eez zis your sohn?*

The long, U-shaped, mahogany bar was packed with Wall Street types and cops, and they cracked up at the statement. For better or worse, Tommy McInerney would be forever known as my "illegitimate son."

In more than ten years as a customer at Rolf's I only ordered one item, *Jaegerschnitzel*. It was a pounded veal cutlet, cooked in a brown mushroom sauce. They could have put the tongue of an old army boot in that sauce and I'd eat it. As Trude handed out menus to our group, she said to me *"Herr Kavanaugh, I dunt know vhy you eefen bozzer wreeding zee menu. You alvays order zee zame zhing,...... Jaegerschnitzel..*

"Und, by zee vay, Chimmy, I vant you to know zhat I vill be goink on facation to Chermany for two veeks.'"

Kidding my old friend I said "Well, Trude, going to visit some of your rich relatives there?"

"Ferry funny, you're zuch a comedian, Chimmy. But eef I came from money, I vood not be vaiting tables een New York; I'd be doink zee Polka een Munich."

"YOU'VE GOT TO DO SOMETHING ABOUT THESE PEOPLE"

A few weeks before, we broke up a knife fight between six junkies in Stuyvesant Park. We had to do hand-to-hand combat to disarm them. Five out of six gave up after some initial "stick work." Number six wanted to fight us with his hunting knife, and was violently dropped by Tommy. Mr. Tough Guy would not walk to the radio car, and went limp, in some half-assed act of civil disobedience. So, we had to drag him to the car. Of course, the local whiners and cop haters had to make their opinions known, once the six men had been disarmed, of course.

A short time later, we were put on notice that we were the targets of a civilian complaint lodged by a person who lived on Rutherford Place, a small street of luxury apartment houses and high priced brownstones. As usual, it was not the knife fighters who complained about their treatment, but a "concerned citizen." Any guy who could have been shot by the cops, and wasn't, usually had no cause for complaint.

I read the complaint and became incensed. The complainant stated that we beat the handcuffed man in the park, then continued to beat him in the radio car. It was a complete lie, and it pissed me off to no end. It never mentioned that the man had a knife.

While we were patrolling in the Stuyvesant Park area, near E. 17th St. and 2nd Avenue, a civilian who looked vaguely familiar hailed us down and started to rant and rail about the junkies and methadonians in Stuyvesant Park: "You've got to do something about *these people*. They are ruining the quality of life for everybody" was his whine.

150

Now, at times, Tommy McInerney could be a little hotheaded, acerbic, and undiplomatic, to put it mildly. There were some neighborhoods where he was not allowed to speak, and the area near Rutherford Place was one of them. I go out of the radio car, and then realized who the guy was. "Aren't you Wellington Hartshorne?" I asked.

"Why, yes I am" he said, with a British accent.

Good Christ, a rich limey prick. The man had a haughty air about him, as if he had money, and his shit didn't stink. All my adult life I was distrustful of a man who had a first name like another guy's last name. It either meant he came from a wealthy family, or had a mother with a weird sense of humor.

"Well, Mr. Hartshorne, aren't you the same man who made the bogus civilian complaint that we beat a prisoner two weeks ago, after we broke up a knife fight in the park?"

"Yes, I wouldn't use the term *bogus*, but I am that person."

"All right, since we now know that you love *these people*, why have you turned on the ones you love?" (I loved sticking it to these phonies).

"You don't understand. I am against all violence."

"Well, well, well. Isn't that just dandy. Mr. Wellington Hartshorne is against all violence in the world. Why, you're a real modern day Matahma Ghandi. Just for the record, I am against violence more than you, since I have to physically engage with these idiots, and you don't. At the first sign of any problem, you can just run into your swanky apartment house and let the doorman take the beating for you, but I can't. And, by the way, my union had to supply me with a lawyer and an investigator. I found out that you admitted to the investigator that you lied in your complaint, and that you only said that the junkie was beaten in the radio car to make sure your complaint was investigated.

"Now, I should sue you for defamation, but since I don't have a career any more, there's nothing to sue for, and I'm sure as hell am not getting out of here any time soon. But, your phony complaint will stay with me forever.

"By the way, Mr. Hartshorne, where do you work?"

"I am a senior Vice-President of Barclay's Bank, in charge of international banking", said Hartshorne.

"Well, Mr. Vice-President, suppose I, who know nothing about the international banking business, just as you know nothing about police work, came into Barclay's Bank and made a complaint against you to your superiors for stealing and misappropriating money, basically calling you a thief. What would be your reaction?"

"I would be outraged, since I am neither a thief, nor a swindler."

"But, maybe, Hartshorne, maybe I want to make sure my complaint gets investigated, since, you see, I am against all dishonesty and thievery in the world. Do you see any similarity here?"

Reflexively, Hartshorne got a bug up his ass and said "I am a respected international banker", as if the prick had a birthright to lie against those he deemed lower than himself on the social scale.

Now I had the little bastard by the balls. "So, it's O.K. to lie to hurt a cop, but not all right to hurt an international banker, right?"

The little worm squirmed, but did not answer.

I was incensed at this puny, elitist snob. "So, why did you lie when you said the prisoner was beaten all the way to the car, and in the car?"

"Look, Mr. Kavanaugh, maybe I embellished a bit to make my complaint look good."

"I'll tell you what, Hartshorne, every day when I drive by here with the windows rolled up, I will be like Sergeant Schultz. 'I vill zee nozzink, I vill hear nozzink, und I vill know nozzink.' And all the other cops who patrol here know what you did. Do you rich people actually think that all of us cops are fucking stupid?"

Mr. Hartshorne sputtered out "But,…..but….. what about my family? They need to be protected. They live in fear every day."

"Well, I fear losing my fucking job because of someone like you. I'm not getting involved in your personal problems. I tried to do that once before, and got screwed for my efforts. You'll have to take care of this yourself. You're a smart man, and you're more educated than me. Just talk to the drug addicts; be kind to them, be sensitive to their needs. And above all, be sure to tell them that you, Wellington Hartshorne, are a man who is against all violence in the world. I'm sure they'll understand.

"Here's what it comes down to. If I drive by and see your wife and kids getting the ever-living shit kicked out of them by one of these zombies, and ignore it, I can always say that I didn't see anything. But, if I am stupid enough to get out of my car and get involved, I can lose my job. Are you starting to get the point now? There are consequences to making false complaints against cops, and one of them is apathy."

"But,... but,... these people are dangerous. We can't even go in our own park"

"Yes, but *you* seem to think that the police are the problem in the park, not the addicts. My revenge for your dishonest civilian complaint will be the thought of you writing out a check to your landlord every month for your prestigious apartment on Rutherford Place. Your rent payment is probably five times more than my mortgage payment for a house in a working class neighborhood. However, when I come out of *my house* every day, all I see is normal, working, law abiding people. What the fuck do *you* see, Hartshorne? You see a pack of dangerous, violent, drug addled losers who would kill you and your entire family in a second just for looking at them funny.

"Your wife and kids can't even walk through the park near your apartment without getting their throats slashed by these scumbags. Wake up to the fact that it's pacifists like you who allow these violent pieces of shit to exist in the world."

In a phony British accent, I concluded the conversation by saying "As we say here in America, old chap, 'payback's a bitch!' Cheerio, I'm off to the hunt."

A society gets the kind of police protection that it deserves. You can call for all of the police review boards, special police prosecutors, and oversight forums that are so slanted and biased against a police officer that he cannot even defend himself from being railroaded. However, cops are not stupid, and there will come a time one day when you call 911, and no one will show up.

It just won't be worth it to go to jail for getting involved in *your problem*.

THE FRISCO DISCO FIASCO

Arnold Levine was ecstatic about having been awarded his first medal, for Meritorious Police Duty, for his role in solving the supermarket homicide. For the first time in his career, he felt like a real cop. Little did he know what the future would hold for him.

Toward the end of the 4 x 12 shift, the dispatcher roared out "13 Charlie-David, respond to the Frisco Disco, 54 East 26th Street, 3rd floor, female calls for help."

Harrison and Levine were there in a matter of seconds. The Frisco Disco was a sado-masochistic, heavy metal rock club, known for kinky sex and violence. They raced up to the third floor and pulled the large door open. As soon as they got past the entrance they heard a woman's screams that sounded like she was being tortured. Suddenly, a bulky, shaven headed, steroid popping goon in a shiny black sweat suit blocked their entrance into the club. Again, they heard the agonizing calls for help.

The bouncer got right in Harrison's face and said "Hey, *brother*, there's a $20 cover charge per person to enter. You better come up with $40.00, or you and your boyfriend a'int getting in here."

Wayne reflexively grabbed this very large, muscle bound man by the testicles in a vicious vice grip. He squeezed the guy's balls so tightly that the man could only speak in a high pitched voice. Harrison said to him "Hey shithead, I a'int your brother, 'cause my mama never had any fuckin' kids who looked like you! I'm a cop, numb-nuts, not a customer. Maybe you didn't get that fucking memo, you weightlifting cocksucker. You can't grow muscles here, can you, fuck-o?"

After ordering the nearly paralyzed man to kneel down, Wayne

155

head butted him, breaking his nose. Then he left him on the floor in the fetal position, holding his aching nuts with one hand, and his bloody nose in the other.

Arnold led the way to the screams and they entered the men's room, only to see a terrible sight: Five leather clad men, with their pants around their ankles, had a skinny young punk rocker woman trapped in a toilet stall, bent over the bowl. One man held her down, while the others took turns raping and anally sodomizing her. The man mounting the victim was the fifth one to violate her.

Now, most of these clubs were no problem—just some weird people having a good time, without being hassled. Yet, there was a small percentage of these clubs where the fringe element came out. The Frisco Disco was one of them. The poor kid getting raped probably rejected the sexual advances of one of the goons, and this was the payback.

The sight of the two cops caused the attackers to fight like maniacs. They knew that if arrested, they would do long prison terms. Harrison managed to get off a quick call for help before the brutal battle engaged. Their five opponents were all muscular men with great strength.

Luckily, men like that are so muscle-bound that they are usually not good fighters, but they still had the potential to hurt a man severely in close quarters.

In the first minute, the two cops valiantly tried to fight off their assailants, but were taking a beating. They stood by the door, blocking the way for the criminals to get out and escape to freedom. The only way they could avoid arrest was to pulverize the two police officers. Arnold and Wayne were running out of steam and could hardly ward off the blows raining down on them any longer.

Just as the battle seemed lost, Tommy and I came on the scene, like the cavalry. Wayne and Arnold did not have time to speak, but we summed up the situation in a second or two. I took one man out with my nightstick, but soon realized the stick would not be useful in the crowded quarters of the bathroom. Tommy knew how to use his slapper, a blackjack-like device without a spring, and smashed one guy's face and eye socket open. The slapper and the blackjack were the old equalizers.

Levine, the nice Jewish boy from Brooklyn, had never been in a fight before in his entire life. He was scared as hell, disoriented and confused. One attacker picked Arnold up by the throat and lifted him off the floor, choking him. Then he took Levine's head and banged it into the wall several times, knocking off his glasses, opening a huge gash on the back of his skull. Having felt intense pain and the warm blood running down his neck, Arnold was filled with a visceral rage that he had never before experienced in his life. He really thought he was going to die.

The fighting was up close and personal, so Arnold took out his blackjack and swung it at his adversary, hitting him square in the forehead three times. Blood gushed out of the man's head like a geyser. Still on adrenaline, Levine, now released from the choke hold, wielded the jack in a roundhouse fashion, and this time struck his opponent in the face, sending him down to the floor with a broken jaw, spitting out blood and teeth onto the white, hexagon tiled floor, now splattered with commingled blood of cops and perps, and the victim's feces (victims of forcible anal sodomy often have uncontrollable bowel movements).

Wayne Harrison was a tough street fighter, originally from the mean streets of Brownsville, Brooklyn. This former Marine had managed to block most of the blows. He had a black eye, and some nasty bruises, but was able to arraign the six prisoners the next morning. Tommy and I were in the same shape. Levine wound up in Bellevue Hospital overnight with several clamps placed in his scalp. The young victim's anus was ripped so badly that it took more than two dozen stitches to repair it.

The interview with the young Assistant District Attorney was most frustrating. Most new A.D.A.'s were assigned to the Complaint Room. There, they interviewed the Police Officers and prepared the criminal complaint for court. Most young assistants were just college kids, who mommy and daddy patted on the ass and sent off to college. They knew nothing of the real world, just the starry-eyed nonsense that their liberal professors had indoctrinated them with in college and law school. Thus, 24 year old A.D.A., Adele Morrissey, could not understand the charge of Rape and Sodomy, First Degree. In her fantasy world, people did not do this to one another, at least not forcibly. Morrissey did not believe Harrison at all, thinking that he was making it all up, perhaps to advance his own career. She challenged Wayne on every aspect of the case, and cynically asked if the victim had, in fact, sustained any injury, or possibly enjoyed it.

Harrison, a proud, religious man, and a good cop, was not one to be politically correct. He had about as much social grace and tact as Tommy McInerney, which is to say, very little. Wayne responded to her taunts by saying. "Listen, honey, the victim was brutally butt-stroked by five huge men. This kid can now bend over at the waist, look up her own asshole, and see the fucking moon at night. Are you starting to get the entire picture now?"

All of the defendants were charged with first degree rape and sodomy, felonious assault and resisting arrest. The bouncer was also charged with Obstructing Governmental Administration for impeding the police rescue efforts. Due the violent nature of the crime, all defendants were remanded without bail.

For their actions in arresting multiple, violent sexual offenders in the act, and engaging in extreme physical combat with the attackers, Levine and Harrison were awarded departmental recognition of "Commendation", the third level of award in the NYPD. Tommy and I received awards for Meritorious Police Duty.

The events of that evening were a great awakening for Arnold Levine. He got his ass kicked, and had a few clamps put in his scalp, but he gave as good as he got, even better. He also found out the hard way that real police work is ugly, dirty, violent, brutal, dangerous, and certainly not glamorous.

158

Levine had never been to the Grand Jury as a street cop. Summoned to testify before the panel, he was nervous. William Moran, a senior Assistant D.A., and the Chief of the Grand Jury Bureau, had taken over the case due to the publicity it generated in the press. Arnold told Moran that he was nervous, and that although he had been a cop for a long time, he had only testified as an expert witness from the Police Lab, not as an arresting officer. Prosecutor Moran was an old pro, and calmed Levine down, telling him to just act like he was telling the story to his family members at the dinner table.

Arnold must have been a great witness, because after he finished testifying, several of the Grand Jurors stood up and applauded. He was bursting with pride, and felt like a real street cop now; he was finally doing something positive for society.

THE TOOTHLESS BANDIT

The future of New York City looked very grim. No bank wanted to cash our paychecks. I had an account at Bankers Trust on E. 23rd Street and 2nd Avenue, but tried to avoid going there. The manager was a snotty, arrogant black woman, Yolanda Bates. She had a chip on her shoulder the size of a railroad tie. I usually cashed my check at the Anawanda Club, but today, I had to put most of my pay into my checking account.

The teller told me that she could not accept a New York City check. When I complained, the teller called Ms. Bates. She snidely said "You need your I.D. card before we can cash your check."

Pointing to the marked radio car out in front of the bank I said "Lady, do you think this is Halloween and I'm in costume?"

Rather that argue with her, I just left, saying to myself "Bitch, you'll need me before I need you."

In the 13th and surrounding Precincts there was an armed robber holding up banks. He was a white junkie with his four front teeth missing. Heroin addicts love sweets, and thus they have a tendency to lose their teeth. His modus operandi was to pull a gun on a bank employee and threaten to shoot them unless he was given money. The robber hit nine banks so far, but had struck only once in our Precinct, on 1st Avenue and E. 14th Street.

A few days later I was still smarting from my humiliation in Bankers Trust, but Ms. Bates was about to get a lesson in payback. About 2:00 P.M. the Toothless Bandit strolled into Bankers Trust, pulled out a .45 automatic pistol and put it to Ms. Bates' head. He announced a holdup, telling the staff that he would shoot the

160

manager if they did not turn over the money.

The robber was temporarily distracted, and Bates ran for the revolving door leading to 2nd Avenue, with the gunman close behind. The Bandit jammed the door with his foot and prevented the manager from exiting, effectively trapping her in the revolving door. Someone managed to call 911, and we got the call of a robbery in progress. We were there in a matter of seconds.

We parked around the corner, and as soon as we observed the robber's missing teeth, I knew that we had our man. His .45 automatic looked very formidable against our .38 caliber revolvers. There was sheer fright and panic in the manager's face; she was screaming wildly, pleading for help. I had to fight to keep from laughing at her plight.

I said "Hold on, Ms. Bates. I have to go back to the station house and get my I.D. card to show to the robber. Don't go anywhere. I'll be right back in a few minutes, O.K."

As I pretended to return to the radio car, Tommy had quietly slipped into the bank via the side entrance. McInerney quietly moved in, and took cover behind a desk, less than ten feet from the robber. He gruffly announced "POLICE, DON'T MOVE!"

The robber let go of his grip on the door, and looked for the source of the command. He quickly saw my partner, but Tommy reduced himself to a small target and had his .38 Smith & Wesson aimed squarely at the man's chest. The robber realized that the police officer had the drop on him, and gave up without a struggle, meekly dropping the gun without a fight.

No cop ever had a problem cashing his check there ever again. However, I would never give that cop hating bitch the satisfaction of going in there, ever again.

IRISH MEETS YIDDISH

At the 4 x 12 roll call, Captain Fitzgerald and Chief Van Der Steig were handing out departmental awards to Levine, Harrison, McInerney and myself for our actions at the Frisco Disco. In attendance in the sitting room was Auxiliary Police Officer Annie Walsh.

Annie had a birth defect that rendered her unable to walk without the aid of heavy metal braces on her legs. She had a very pretty face, nice body, and a great personality. She was never bitter about her handicap. Her family did not bother with her, and she lived off of Social Security disability and a trust fund from her late father, a wealthy Wall Street banker. Because of her physical limitations, she could not go on patrol, but worked inside doing typing and filing. Annie was very well-liked in the 13th Precinct, and the Police Department had become her surrogate family.

All of her life people were condescending to her because she was crippled. In the NYPD, it was not the same. She was treated like everyone else and loved it. If you were someone who wanted sympathy, a New York City police station was not the place for you. Like most of the cops, she had a nickname. Hers was "Wonder Woman", because of her metal legs.

Annie had never spoken to Arnold Levine, but she went up to Arnold and congratulated him on his Commendation. Arnold liked her from the get-go. Soon, they were smitten with each other. Levine was a shy man, who at age 36 had never married.

When he was 21 years old, he was pushed into a half-assed, arranged marriage with the daughter of his father's business partner.

162

Arnold did not go through with the marriage, and that led to his estrangement from his parents. He last saw them at his uncle Marvin's funeral, but they did not speak. His shyness broke down around Annie. She was such a lovely person it was very easy to talk to her. Levine broke through his wall of shyness. Since he was off the next day, he asked Annie for a date. She gladly accepted. Arnold said to himself "I'm glad I am estranged from my parents. What if they knew I was dating a *goy*?"

THE GREATEST GENERATION
GIVES ADVICE

About 9:00 P.M. we got called to a fire at on East 17th Street, on the 2nd floor. We were only two blocks away. Being veteran cops, we knew enough to park away from the building, and not to block any fire hydrants. We could see the smoke coming out from the front window and underneath the door. The tenant had several strong locks on the door to keep the junkies out. We heard agonizing screams coming from inside the apartment. It was the occupant being slowly burned to death.

The man was a paraplegic who smoked in bed. His cigarette fell onto the mattress, and started a fire. Tommy raced to the radio car to get the tire iron. I could not push the door open, even kicking it with all of my strength. There was no fire escape either. It was gut wrenching to hear the dying man's screams for help, but we were unable to do anything. The frustration was unbearable.

The NYFD arrived in a few minutes. Even with their heavy equipment, it took them some time to open the door. The fire was confined to the bed and quickly put out, but it was too late for the victim. I turned away, rather than look at the burned corpse, but Tommy did, out of some curious, morbid feeling. The man looked like a marshmallow that was kept on the barbecue too long.

The smell of burnt human flesh was as bad as a decayed cadaver. Death by fire is a horrible way to go, and I respected the NYFD firefighters for the dangerous job that they did, day in and day out. The pitiful, agonizing screams of the victim would haunt me in my dreams for many years. Decades later, I would still wake up saturated with sweat after reliving this nightmare, over and over,

164

always anguished that I could do nothing to help the man.

With every nightmare, I would see myself and McInerney standing in the hallway, helpless, while the victim cried out to us to save him. What the hell could I have done differently? I know that I can look God in the eye and say that I did my best to help the man. But, it was still a painful burden to carry through life.

While Tommy went to the Anawanda Club after work, I begged off, and went to my neighborhood bar, the North Star. There was a good mix of local people there, with many cops, firemen, sanitation workers, construction men, and military veterans. After a couple of beers, I started talking to retired NYPD Police Officer, Billy Burke, a World War II veteran, and deeply religious man.

Billy was a highly respected man, and an idol for many of us Baby Boomers in town. In World War II, Burke spent three years as an infantryman in North Africa and Europe, from age 17 to 20. At an age when most guys are finishing high school and going to college, Billy battled his way through hell in north Africa and Europe. He came home in 1945, raised a family, and served honorably as a police officer in Staten Island's 120th Precinct.

I still called him "Mr. Burke" out of a profound respect, as did my peers. A sympathetic listener, Billy heard my story about the man burned to death, and my frustration about not being able to help him.

He said "Listen, Jimmy, I've seen some nasty sights in my lifetime. Just remember that there are some things in this life that you can change, and some that you can't. You just have to ask God for the wisdom to know the difference. Otherwise, you'll just go out of your fucking mind."

Mr. Burke's advice was just what I needed.

FARMER IN THE CITY

The George Washington Hotel on E. 23rd St. and Lexington Avenue was a decent place. Some of the larger rooms were rented by long term tenants, some of whom had been there for thirty years or more. An elderly woman called the Precinct one day and told Lt. von Richter that someone in the nearby Kenmore Hotel was growing marijuana in his room.

We were assigned the job by the desk officer. After a few knocks on the door, a 70ish woman opened up and greeted us by saying "The man across the way is growing marijuana. It looks like a big operation."

She pointed to a room on the tenth floor of the Kenmore, about fifty or sixty feet away. "Do you see that ultra violet light in the window? Well, look past it, and you can see the marijuana plants in the room."

I was initially skeptical, thinking that she just an old busybody, with nothing else to do. From what I could see, however, she could be right. We just needed some more proof. Sure enough, the old lady had a pair of eight power binoculars.

Looking through them, I could see that she was correct in her observations. The marijuana plants were over six feet tall. Counting from the right, the suspect's room was the sixth one from the Lexington Avenue side of the building. We told the desk clerk at the Kenmore that there was a call about a prowler on the roof, so he wouldn't tip off the suspect. We got to the tenth floor and counted six rooms from left to right, leading us to room 1010.

As we approached the suspect's room in the dimly lit, carpeted hallway, the pungent smell of marijuana came out from under the door. It was so thick you could almost cut it. The odor was so overpowering that we had to breathe through our handkerchiefs. Upon knocking, the tenant opened the door, and we could see a virtual forest of cannabis plants in plain view. All I could say to the guy was "You're under arrest………."

The spaced out fool said "Well, I guess it's for my floral arrangement."

Some floral arrangement! There were marijuana plants with stalks as thick as a broomstick, and enough to fill a paddy wagon and two radio cars.

The arraignment was something else. Tommy took the collar and went to Night Court. There he locked horns with the Criminal Court judge, a former Legal Aid Society lawyer, and political clubhouse hack (pardon the redundancy), Lester Levitt. This judge used the bench as his personal soap box to advocate for criminals. He read the complaint, and lashed out at McInerney, accusing him of home invasion, kidnapping, and illegal search and seizure.

The defendant's brain had been burned out from drugs over the years. The judge asked the prisoner this leading question: "Didn't the police burst into your apartment and look around to find the marijuana plants?"

The man truthfully answered "Hell, no, Judge, You could see and smell them right from the front door. I had a goddam marijuana forest in there." After making what is called a "judicial admission", i.e. an incriminating statement made in open court, the defendant had just butt-fucked himself real good, in the legal sense. Levitt called both attorneys to the bench for a conference. When counsel returned to their respective places, the defendant took a plea to misdemeanor possession of marijuana, and accepted a six month sentence. Tommy said to himself "Fuck you, Levitt, and your Liberal Aid Society, too."

WILD BILL'S BLUNDER

Jack Van Pelt and Fred "Mr. Wizard" Davidovich made a terrific reputation for themselves in the Gramercy Park Precinct in just a short time. Using their accumulated knowledge, they saved lives and assisted dozens of people over the summer.

The partners have talked emotionally disturbed people from jumping off roof tops, saved gunshot victims, given CPR, rescued a man from certain death by electrocution, and made half a dozen gun collars.

The call to the George Washington Hotel on E. 23rd Street, was typical for them: "13 Eddie-Frank, respond to the roof of the George Washington Hotel, report of a possible jumper." We were assigned as their back-up.

Right after acknowledging receipt of the job, we heard Sgt. Hanley say "13 Sergeant also responding."

Mr. Wizard reflexively said "This fool will wind up killing the guy."

Just as Sector Eddie-Frank arrived at the hotel, they heard Hanley's voice telling the dispatcher to advise the two radio car crews to wait for him before going to the roof.

Davidovich acknowledged the request and angrily slammed down the mike.

Steaming, we waited for Wild Bill, who came in like a bull in a china shop. Upon arriving on the roof we observed a blonde man in his early twenties, who was sitting on the parapet facing the street. He was dangling his legs over the edge and smoking a cigarette.

He wore a tan suede western jacket with fringes, black cowboy hat, and was obviously very disturbed and agitated. Van Pelt had handled many jumpers before, and knew what to do and say. We held back and let Jack do his thing.

Hanley, on the other hand, could only exacerbate the situation, through ignorance and brain damage, due to a lifetime of alcohol abuse. Basically, Will Bill could screw up a one car funeral. However, due to NYPD rules, Hanley was in charge.

After talking to the man for a few minutes, Jack offered him a cigarette, which he accepted. Van had built up a rapport with the younger man, and was just about to reach out and grab him, and bring him back to safety.

Hanley was getting impatient and said to the would-be jumper "You know what the problem here is, pal? You just don't have the fucking balls to kill yourself. You're like all of the other publicity hounds who want to see their picture in the Daily News tomorrow.

"We don't have all day, and I'm not paying these guys overtime just to get in some kind of circle-jerk with you on this rooftop. So, you either jump now, or surrender." With that, the troubled young man told Jack to back off, and flicked his cigarette off of the roof onto Twenty-third Street. He walked about twenty-five feet from the edge of the building and removed his jacket and hat. He gave a final look at Van Pelt and flashed him a faint smile, then turned, and sprinted toward the street. Using the parapet to spring off of, he jumped and fell seventeen stories, landing head first through the windshield of a westbound Cadillac sedan. There was nothing left of the kid's head, as his skull, brains and blood exploded all over the elderly driver and passenger.

The eighty-two year old male passenger died instantly of a heart attack, and the driver went into deep shock.

It was a terrible tragedy, and yet, just another classic Hanley *clusterfuck*. Nobody said anything about it, and the cops wrote it off as just another story in the Naked City. Wild Bill had this Alfred E. Newman, *What, me worry?*, look on his face.

Jack Van Pelt was despondent and disgusted. After all of his years in the Emergency Service Division he had never lost one jumper. It took a jerk like Hanley to wind up killing the kid, and someone else. For his efforts in botching a routine rescue, Sgt. "Wild Bill" Hanley was awarded the 13th Precinct's *Asshole of The Month* award, for conspicuous stupidity and incredibly poor judgment in causing the death of an emotionally disturbed young man and an innocent bystander. He was a frequent recipient of this dubious award.

They say that doctors bury their mistakes. Well, sometimes cops do too.

METHADONE MADNESS

My sectors, Adam-Boy, had over 25 methadone clinics on the east side. It attracted hundreds of the criminal element to an otherwise nice neighborhood. Basically, the methadone program began when the underbelly of the medical profession and the bottom feeders of the social service industry realized that they could make a lot of money from other people's personal weaknesses. They put the program in a nice package, and called it "drug treatment" so they could insulate themselves from criticism, while reaping a financial windfall at the taxpayers' expense.

Most heroin users have to shoot up about three times a day to keep their high. Methadone is a synthetic opiate more powerful than heroin, that is taken orally in liquid form, once a day. In theory, the methadone was to keep the addict stupefied so that he didn't steal to support his habit. In reality, the program was a disaster. The addicts' handlers hadn't factored in their irresponsible behavior, and inherent self-destructive personalities. The unsuspecting public did not grasp the greed of the medical whores and poverty pimps who were administering these programs. Without proper support and supervision, the methadone program soon deteriorated into a vast cesspool of fraud. The clinics handed out their doses of methadone in the morning. In one of the more disgusting aspects of the program, junkies would drink the meth in the clinic, but not swallow it. Then they would go outside and spit the methadone into a cup and sell it to some schumck from Jersey. It was called "spit-back." Incredibly, every weekday morning, they were dozens of morons lined up outside the clinics to buy cups of spit-back.

On Fridays, the clinics gave the addicts their Saturday and

171

Sunday doses to take home. Most sold it on the street, then reported that they were robbed. The money they received was used to purchase other drugs. The clinics' owners were making money, so they didn't care. They all lived in exclusive neighborhoods somewhere else, and got paid by the head. The more junkies coming through their front door, the easier it was to make the payments on their BMW or Mercedes-Benz.

Put a number of useless, idle, spaced-out drug users in a given location, and you will soon have trouble. The clinic at E. 26th Street and 2nd Avenue was no exception. It was run by a doctor named Mortensen. He had ruined the quality of life in the area by operating the clinic in a reckless manner. His *patients* were unsupervised troublemakers. But, at the end of the day, Dr. Mortensen drove off in his BMW and returned home to his condo in Englewood Cliffs, New Jersey, with a beautiful view of the Manhattan skyline.

Over the summer we had few run-ins with Dr. Mortensen, so the current condition was no surprise. The owner of a Greek diner next to the clinic called the police to complain of the thirty to forty methadonians blocking the entrance to his front door.

When we arrived, they reluctantly moved on. Dr. Mortensen came out and started to publicly berate us. "If you keep hassling my patients, I'll make a civilian complaint against you."

I was in no mood to be threatened by this quack. "First of all, these worthless pieces of crap are not *patients*. A *patient* is a sick person who is under a doctor's care and getting medical treatment. These people are not sick. They have a self-inflicted disability that *you* are only making worse. Doctor, you and I both know that this whole program is one big crock of shit. It's like claiming to help a wino by giving him a bottle of scotch every day – then sending the tab to the taxpaying suckers. The only thing that changed is that you made a lot of money off of these pathetic people."

Mortensen was incensed. "What do you know about drug treatment? Do you have a medical degree?"

"I may only be a cop, but I have not had a full frontal lobotomy. This is not drug treatment. These mopes are just as fucked up today as the first day they walked into your clinic. Any normal person can see what is going on here. You screw up a nice neighborhood, then drive over the bridge to your condo in Jersey, and leave us to clean up the mess you created."

Actually, I had run Mortensen's license plate and found his address. I called my Army buddy who was a cop in Englewood Cliffs for the scoop on the building; it was a 'big bucks' place.

Mortensen barked "I'll have your job for spying on me!"

I shot back "You're going to fuck me? I don't think so. You're the one who's going to be grabbing his ankles. All I have to do is make one complaint to the New York State Department of Health, and your whole jack-off, bullshit empire will fold like a cheap tent. If you want to play games, I guarangoddamntee you that this place will be locked up tighter than a clam's ass. So, you have two choices. You can start supervising your people, or the state will shut you down. It's your decision."

Bringing in the Health Department was the last resort. I knew in my heart that the program was a total scam, but it employed nurses, clerical people, psychologists, and others. Why cause some underlings to lose their jobs because their boss was a jerk? Mortensen got the message, and cleaned up his act. He hired a security guard to make his *patients* move on, and not loiter in the area. I saw it as a minor victory for civilization.

NUMB NUTS NOONAN'S
LAST HURRAH

Sgt. Jane Parker was the day shift supervisor, and her driver was 61 year old Cornelius "Numb Nuts" Noonan. Just after they passed Union Square Park, heading westbound on 17th Street, a call came over the radio announcing an armed robbery at Citibank, 17th Street and 5th Avenue. Parker responded that they were going. She and Neil were less than a block away.

As they approached the scene, two young Hispanic men came running out of the bank, each holding a bag of stolen cash. One ran north, and the other ran south on 5th Avenue. Parker took off on foot after the southbound suspect. Neil chased his man up 5th Avenue, against traffic, skillfully weaving in and out of traffic, until he finally overtook him at 21st Street. The old time cop drove the radio car onto the sidewalk and cut off the fleeing suspect, blocking his escape.

As the robber pretended to give up, he reached around, took out a bayonet, and plunged it into Neil's upper chest. The weapon entered right where the shoulder is attached to the body, and came out the other side. Without hesitation, Noonan blasted his attacker with three rounds square in the chest, killing him instantly. Numb Nuts may have had dementia, but the man wasn't stupid. It was the first time in thirty-nine years that he had fired his revolver in the line of duty. Neil was in extreme pain, made worse for the fact that the bayonet pierced his body right where he had been wounded in World War II.

More units arrived on the scene. Sgt. Parker caught her prisoner and disarmed him of an automatic pistol. A radio car took Noonan directly to Bellevue. The operation to remove the weapon took several hours, but Neil would make a full recovery.

Captain Fitzgerald visited Numb Nuts in the hospital as he was recovering, and said to him "How are you feeling, Neil?"

The wounded man replied "Pretty good, Cap', considering. You know, if Rommel and the Afrika Korps couldn't do me in, no two-bit bank robber will either, Skip'."

The Captain continued "I'm glad you're O.K. now. You know, *Numbie*, you've got to realize that it's a young man's job out there today. Maybe it's time to put your papers in. After all, you're sixty-one fucking years old."

"Yeah, Skipper, I think you're right. This *is* a young man's job, and I'm just too damn old for it."

The NYPD was Neil Noonan's whole life, and he was tormented that it would soon be all over. However, he went out with a bang, receiving the Medal of Honor, the NYPD's highest award.

TUNNEL VISION

The double parked red '72 Dodge Charger on 2nd Avenue, between E. 18th and E. 19th Streets seemed out of place to us. One of the elements to being a good cop is knowing what was normal for the neighborhood, and what was not. A car outside a liquor store just before 10 o'clock at night might be innocent enough, but we knew that this store catered to local people, mainly Manhattan cliff-dwellers, who did not own cars. It started to look damn suspicious to us.

We held back a block, on the opposite side of the street. The liquor store was the only business open on the block, and we had a good view of the store entrance. It was owned by Irv Cohen and his wife, Celia. Irv was a nice old guy, who was a World War II veteran, having served in the U.S. Army Signal Corps in France and Germany. He literally had a 'mom and pop' store. I had stopped there on occasion, just to introduce myself, on the few occasions I had foot patrol. Irv liked me because I was also an Army veteran, and he loved to tell his Army stories, and listen to mine.

All of a sudden, we heard what sounded like a gunshot, as two long haired white males ran out of the liquor store and got into the Charger. The driver peeled out, and turned westbound on 17th Street, then north on 3rd Avenue, leaving the aroma of burnt Michelins behind.

We took off in pursuit and tried to stay on his tail, but our Plymouth Fury was no match for the souped-up Charger. We radioed for a unit to check the liquor store, and for other units to block the fleeing vehicle on 3rd Avenue.

Harrison and Levine in sector Charlie-David tried to block the suspects at 29th Street, but the slick wheelman whipped to the left, then to the right, passing the radio car like it was invisible. At 36th Street, the pursued vehicle turned eastbound, and we now realized they were making their break for Queens, to escape via the Queens-Midtown Tunnel. The dispatcher was alerted to have the tunnel closed on the Queens side.

The Charger got slowed down in traffic, and we caught up to it in the tunnel. Even with our roof lights blazing, and our siren wailing, these guys were not stopping.

We resorted to playing " bumper cars" with the Dodge, but it still would not stop. As we got into the middle of the tunnel, the driver of the Charger lost control and began to ride on two wheels, with the other two wheels riding on the wall. Tiles were shooting off of the wall, pelting our radio car with a shower of ceramic shards.

While we correctly suspected a holdup, what we didn't know at the time was that Irv had been shot.

As we came within view of the Queens side, the Triboro Bridge and Tunnel Police had done a good job in setting up a roadblock for us. Our amateur robbers gave up without a fight, and surrendered their murder weapon, a .357 Colt Python. They had robbed Irv's store and were heading home to the Flushing section of Queens.

The two gunmen were brought back to the store, where a distraught Celia positively identified them both in a show-up. They were worthless junkies, looking for a quick score.

Irv Cohen would survive the shooting, but he would eventually give up the store. On the way home that night, I said to myself "Does this fucking job ever bring any good news?"

CAROLINA OUTRAGE

After handling a job at Broadway and 29th Street, a fat woman with three kids in tow hailed us down. She had an arrogant attitude when she approached the radio car. Her first words were "Take me to this address" as she showed us a letter from the South Carolina Department of Social Services. McInerney read the letter first, and began to turn purple with rage, like I had never seen the man. Fatso and her three children were given one way bus tickets from South Carolina to New York City. Her letter of instruction was for her to flag down the nearest cab and demand to be taken to the New York City Emergency Welfare Center at 241 Church Street. The letter said that the City of New York would pay for the taxi ride.

Once there, she was told to demand an apartment for herself and her dependents. If they had to put her up in a hotel, she was to demand meal vouchers, since she had no kitchen. Of course, she should sign up for food stamps, and a welfare check, too. Tommy, who was now working for a landscaper on the side, looked at the woman, and in a fit of anger said "You've got to be kidding me lady! I'm working two jobs so someone like you can just come up here and live off of the working people of New York City? Go back to Carolina and get a job, you lazy bum!"

Tommy kept the letter because nobody would believe him otherwise. Here we were, living in a bankrupt city that could no longer pay its bills; we were reduced to cashing our paychecks in a bar, working two, and three jobs, and the losers in charge of New York City were still attracting more welfare recipients. It was as if the inmates were running the insane asylum. The City of New York had gone bankrupt by trying to provide for every parasitic human being who came into its borders. Yet, here it was, still luring poverty cases to The Big Apple. Having hundreds of thousands of people like this one coming to bankrupt New York City was like throwing an anvil to a drowning man.

Of course, this woman, and many like her, would never leave as long as they continued to get their handouts. The vast social service industry of New York City fed off of people like this, and it needed them. The more dependent people they took care of, the more the Department of Social Services budget will be for the next year. No matter that New York City had gone bust and could not pay its bills, nor its police; just keep the crop of unproductive people coming to feed the social service giant.

Back in the radio car, my partner was still steaming. We had our salaries cut, and were moonlighting, doing menial work, just to stay alive. Yet, tax money that could have been used to pay us a decent wage was being used wastefully on people who had no stake in this city. They just came to leech off of the New York City taxpayer. McInerney blurted out "You know, Jimmy, my cousin used to say that New York City was living proof that the South really won the Civil War. They have all of our factories, and we have all their welfare recipients."

"Ain't that the fuckin' truth", I chimed in.

SCHIZO, SPLITZO

As I was finishing a day shift, I got a call at work from the South Beach Psychiatric Center in Staten Island. My brother Frank suffered from schizophrenia, and was being treated there. He escaped from the hospital, and could not be found. This had happened before, and I always found him at the Whitehall slip of the Staten Island Ferry Terminal, or in the St. George Terminal on the Staten Island side.

Getting off work at 4:00 P.M., I headed downtown to the Manhattan terminal of the ferry. Frank was not there, so I rode the boat over to Staten Island. He was not at St. George, either. On a hunch, I went back to Manhattan and drove up to the Bowery, and found him standing in front of the Men's Shelter at 8 E. 3rd Street. This pathetic shell of a man had been beaten, bloodied, and robbed of what little money and dignity that he had.

Upon seeing my brother I broke down in my car, banging the steering wheel and cursing God for doing this to Frank. It took a few minutes before I could compose myself enough to get out of the car. I gently approached Frank so as not to spook him. "Frank, it's Jimmy. Come with me. You can't stay here, it's too dangerous for you."

Frank looked at me with this blank stare, but underneath that façade, I could tell that inside of him there was someone trying to reach out to me, but who was not able to communicate. My brother barely recognized me, the one person in the world who was the closest to him.

"Frank, I can't help you, but the people at South Beach can. Come with me and I'll take you back. I know it's not a nice place, but you have only one chance to get better. You're just not safe

180

here"

I knew in my heart that Frank would never get better. He climbed into the front seat of my car and did not fight at all. The sadness of losing my brother to this dreaded disease was overwhelming. Why the hell did this have to happen to my brother? He was perfectly normal until age nineteen. "Why?".... I asked God, over and over, as I bitterly cursed Him to myself. There was no answer... and there would never be any answer.

After returning Frank to South Beach, I got back to my car and broke down crying again. It is a wonderful thing to have a brother, but quite terrible to lose him to mental illness. It broke my heart and crushed my spirit as a man. At every Christmas, birthday party, Thanksgiving dinner, summer barbecue, and Super Bowl party, there would always be that empty chair and a heartbroken family that was never the same.

Mental illness is the cruelest of diseases. If you lose an eye or a limb, you can still enjoy life. But, if you lose your mind, your life might as well be over.

For those who don't know the value of a brother, just ask a guy who lost one.

ESCAPE FROM DEATH

The years of grueling patrol duty and the loss of my brother Frank to mental illness had left me, a once religious man, as not quite an atheist, but a man who just didn't give a damn about religion or God any more. I saw so much hate, cruelty, injustice and barbarism in my daily work that I often doubted the existence of God. Put this all together, and you had a guy who had just lost his faith in everything.

We got a call to a methadone clinic one morning. There was a meth patient who was having a mental breakdown. The EMT's had him in a wheelchair and were trying to tie his hands down, to stop his arms from flailing. They asked us for help in restraining the man. Just as I leaned over to hold the man's hand, he grabbed my revolver and violently wrenched it from my holster. In an instant, my own .38 caliber Smith & Wesson revolver was pressed into my chest, and the crazed man was pulling back on the trigger.

Luckily, I had great training, and immediately knew what to do. I wrapped my left hand tightly around the cylinder, which kept the hammer from coming forward. With my right hand, I used all of my strength to pull the gun toward the man's thumb. The revolver popped out of his hand and I re-holstered my weapon. The entire incident lasted about two seconds, but I thought that I was going to die. Just like the time at the Elton Hotel, I had a flashback from an incident. This time it was from 1949, when I was three years old, and had run away from home. I was lost and very scared. My older brother found me a half a mile away.

Tommy assumed that I would collar the guy for attempted grand larceny. But, I had sympathy for the mentally ill, and could not do it. The EMT's said that they would not rat if I 'tuned the guy up' a bit in the ambulance, since he deserved it. I thanked them, but declined without any explanation.

McInerney knew a little about my schizophrenic brother, but not a lot.

However, he knew enough to not press the issue. One of the things about being a good friend and partner was to know when to keep your mouth shut, and when to speak.

BAD NEWS

I hadn't called my old partner, Ben Harrigan, for a few weeks, and it was odd for him not to call me. I wasn't very worried, because I thought he was out looking for a job. He left a good position with a Wall Street brokerage firm to become a cop, but they would not take him back. The City of New York hired these men and women, trained them in the Police Academy, and then laid them off due to the politicians' fiscal and personal irresponsibility.

Most of the laid off men and women left better paying jobs, but wanted to be cops and serve the public as their defenders. The City left them high and dry, with no severance pay, and worst of all, no medical insurance, as of August 31st.

When I called Ben's apartment in Bay Ridge, his mother, Kathleen, answered the phone. From the tone of her voice, I knew something was wrong,

"Mrs. Harrigan, it's Jimmy Kavanaugh. How are you?"

"Jimmy, I was going to call you. Ben is not well. He is in Sloan-Kettering Hospital."

Upon hearing those words, I felt like the world just caved in on me. Sloan-Kettering was a world famous cancer treatment hospital. I had lost my brother to another disease, and now this bad news about Ben.

"Kathleen, what's going on?"

"Ben was feeling tired and weak all the time. He went to the doctor for tests and his white blood count was very high, and Doctor Rosen sent him to Sloan-Kettering. He was diagnosed with leukemia. The doctors there said that he has a treatable form of the

184

disease."

I found it hard to speak, so Kathleen filled in the gaps. "You know, Jimmy, Ben will have no health insurance after August 31st. There are treatments available, but, even with insurance, we already have thousands of dollars in co-payments that are due. Ben's father was a trackman for the Transit Authority who was killed on the job ten years ago. We have nothing."

"Kathleen, I'll do what I can do. And tell Ben that I will be over to see him soon."

At the next roll call, I got up in front of the platoon and told them about young Ben Harrigan's plight. We passed the hat, and collected over three hundred dollars from guys who were living from check to check, and working two jobs. The detective squad gave as much, and I stayed to address the other platoons, who also donated. The Emergency Service cops next door came through, big time.

In the summer of 1975, I had the grand total of $2,000.00 in the bank. With my wife's consent, I withdrew half of it and gave it to Mrs. Harrigan. Mr. McSorley gave $200.00, without batting an eye. Altogether, I was able to give Kathleen over $2,500.00. However, after visiting Ben in the hospital, one doctor told me that the treatments could cost tens of thousands of dollars, maybe even more, without insurance. If only Ben could keep his medical insurance a few months longer.

CALLING IN A FAVOR

I met with our union delegate, 'Loud Lenny' Lantini. As you may recall, Lantini was the man who negotiated with Mr. McSorley about cashing our paychecks at his bar. The loss of medical insurance was a great blow to the young cops who were abruptly laid off. The P.B.A. had alerted its lobbyist in Albany to extend medical benefits for its laid off members, but the proposed bill was languishing in the Civil Service Committee.

Recalling that Mr. Terrence Crowley, (the Electrolux-loving attorney) was counsel to Assemblyman J. Stewart Lovell, we decided to pay him a visit. We drove over to his 14th Street office, entered the reception area, and spoke to the secretary.

"Police Officers Kavanaugh and McInerney here to see Mr. Crowley."

A moment later the secretary came out and said "I'm sorry, Mr. Crowley is busy at the moment. You'll have to come back at a later time."

I knew we were being jerked off, so I said "Go back in and tell Mr. Crowley it's the two police officers who helped him out with his vacuum cleaner problem."

Within seconds we were ushered into the attorney's office. The man had a sheepish look on his face, but he greeted us warmly.

I spoke first. "Mr. Crowley, we are here on behalf of the five thousand police officers of the NYPD who were laid off on June 30th by the City of New York. They will have no medical insurance as of August 31st. Can you help them?"

Crowley started to tap dance around the issue. "You know, gentlemen, that's an expensive item. It's going to be hard to sell this to the upstate people. You know how much they hate New York City. They look at us like a giant welfare sink-hole that their tax money gets poured into. We have a pending bill, but it's stalled in committee"

Having done my homework, I knew that Assemblyman Lovell was the Chairman of the Civil Service Committee, and was *the man* to get things done in Albany.

I went for broke. "Mr. Crowley, there are only four other people on this earth who know that you were humpin' your Hoover. Can we keep this number at four, sir?"

Crowley looked worried, and said "I'll see what I can do for you."

LOVELL'S THE MAN

Assemblyman Lovell was in Albany at the time. Crowley drove up there in record time. Without giving anything away about his appliance affair, he presented the problem of the lack of medical insurance to his boss, who called an emergency meeting of the Assembly. Lovell was a big time mover and shaker, and saw this as an opportunity to help the laid off cops. He made a passionate plea to the members of the Assembly to pass a bill to extend the medical insurance for laid off police officers, for six more months.

The State Senate got wind of Lovell's bill, and not to be outdone, immediately came into session to pass it unanimously. It was signed into law a few days later.

The police unions named Assemblyman Lovell "Man of the Year." He had received that distinction several times before for his good work on our behalf, but it would never be appreciated more than this time.

GOOD NEWS

Lenny Lantini phoned Mrs. Harrigan to tell her that the medical insurance would last six more months, by an act of the New York State Legislature. Kathleen was ecstatic. That would be just what Ben needed to complete his treatments.

If she had only known that this happened because some lawyer was giving himself a knobber with a vacuum cleaner hose! Well, as Shakespeare wrote "All's well that ends well."

THE DYNAMIC DUO

Freddie Zarullo was the only one working in the 13th Precinct Detective Unit that day. He asked Lt. Cantorwicz if he could borrow someone from patrol, in case he had to go out on a case. Uncle Carl told Arnold Levine to work with Zarullo for the day.

Zarullo was killing time, looking through his open case files, when he received a phone call to go to 444 2nd Avenue, apartment 16-J. The message was that there was a homicide in the apartment. When they got there, the uniformed cops told Freddie that the dead guy was married to a woman named Yolanda. She was having an affair for many years with a man named Jose Carrera, and wanted to break off the relationship. Carrera would not end it graciously. He was insane with jealousy, after having caught her with her husband.

Freddie quickly summed it up as the basic machismo-idiot homicide. It would not be a routine investigation, however, because witnesses reported seeing Carrera forcing Yolanda and her young daughter into a car at gunpoint. The Department of Motor Vehicles had no record of a Jose Carrera owning a car. So now, Levine and Zarullo had a dead body, two kidnapping victims being held somewhere, with no leads.

The obvious place to look for Carrera was at his Brooklyn apartment, but Freddie's gut reaction was that the guy would not be that stupid. From his days in the Police Lab, Levine had a keen eye for detail. He observed a note pad on a small table next to the telephone. The Manhattan phone book was nearby, and opened. It looked like the killer had looked up someone's phone number, wrote it on the note pad and ripped out the page. It would take hours to track down everyone on the two pages of the phone book.

Arnold had an idea. He found a pencil, held it sideways, and gently slid the pencil over the note pad. Sometimes, the impression from the paper being written on will come through onto the next page. Patiently, he gently maneuvered the pencil over the paper, and seven numbers came up, and it looked like a phone number: "673-8983."

Freddie grabbed the phone book and used his index finger to slowly go down the page, looking at each telephone number until he found it. The number belonged to a Roberto Rosario, who lived on Rivington Street in the 7th Precinct.

With two lives on the line, Freddie could not take any chances putting this information over the police radio, in case the suspect had a police scanner. He called down to the 7th Pct. Detective Squad, and told them that he may have a murder suspect and two kidnapping victims holed up in an apartment on Rivington Street. It was a low-life, junkie-infested neighborhood.

With Levine driving, they barreled down the F.D.R. Drive, and were around the corner from the seedy apartment building in less than ten minutes. There, they were met by two 7th P.D.U. detectives, Miguel Cruz and Carmelo Manobianco. Freddie knew them, but Levine did not. The local detectives knew the building well. It was a railroad flat, meaning that the apartment was a straight run from front to back, with all of the rooms off of the hallway.

Cruz took off his jacket and tie so that he could fit into the neighborhood. But, to the street-wise punks in this crime infested area, his name just might as well have been Paddy O'Brien. He walked up to the building to check it out. The super, a man named George, told him that Roberto Rosario lived on the third floor. He had seen him come in earlier with his cousin, Jose, a woman, and a young girl, and had not seen them leave. Cruz told the super not to talk to anyone.

The detectives met and listened to what Det. Cruz had to say. It was Zarullo's case, so they deferred to him to figure out how to get into the apartment without anyone getting hurt. Freddie thought for a bit, and said "Let's go, boys", as he went over the plan on the way to the building.

Zarullo knocked on the door and a man's voice inside said "*Wha choo wan', main?*"

Freddie, trying unsuccessfully to speak in a Spanish accent, said "It's George, the super. There's a gas leak. You have to leave the apartment right now."

With that, the door opened, and it was Jose Carrera, the killer. He took one look at Levine and Zarullo and made them as cops. Freddie put his foot in the doorway, and they pushed hard on the door. Arnold tackled the man as soon as he got in. The suspect was now face down on the foyer floor, trying to reach the 9 mm. automatic pistol that was tucked into his waistband.

While Levine struggled with the more powerful suspect, Zarullo did the *tarantella* on Carrera's head, causing him to let go of his hold on the pistol. Cruz and Manobianco grabbed the 9 mm. and helped Levine cuff the suspect.

Once their man was subdued, Freddie warned the other detectives that there may be another man in there, Rosario. The woman and her daughter were found gagged and tied up in a bedroom. They pointed to the room where the other man was.

Cautiously, Cruz and Manobianco opened a closet door, and there was Roberto Rosario, holding a sawed-off shotgun. He would not let go of the weapon until he was given an attitude adjustment by the detectives, in the form of a blackjack applied to his skull.

This was a tremendous collar, and Freddie could coast for a while, living off of the dividends of these two arrests. The major newspapers gobbled up the story, and Sgt. Herring would have to eat a massive helping of crow as a main course, along with a yard of his own shit for an appetizer.

Zarullo's *rabbi* on the job was Lt. Enzo Caruso, who worked as the aide to the Chief of Detectives. Although Zarullo was not Italian, he played in the Columbian Society band. Caruso played the clarinet, and Freddie played the drums. As long as Lt. Caruso was the power behind the throne, Freddie was untouchable, and his bosses knew it. Such was the state of NYPD politics.

ARNOLD POPS THE QUESTION

Arnold and Annie went out for dinner that evening, and he recounted the events of the day for her. Annie was a good listener, and Arnold loved to be in her company. Simply put, Arnold had fallen head over heels in love with Annie Walsh. Although Annie held her cards close to her vest, she realized that she also loved Arnold.

Even though they were different religious and ethnic backgrounds, they both had much in common. The main thing was that they were both estranged from their families. Arnold's estrangement was for defying his parents on the arranged marriage, and Annie because of her rigid, snobbish, lace curtain Irish mother and siblings who could not accept the fact that they had a less than perfect daughter and sister.

The couple went out to dinner at Molly Malone's on 3rd Avenue, near the Precinct. Annie looked great, and she wore an ankle length skirt to hide her braces. After dinner, they walked back to her apartment on East 22nd Street. After drinks, they sat on the couch cuddling and kissing. Arnold knew that this was the woman for him. He wondered if she would ever agree to marry a Jewish man.

This was all new to Annie. No man had ever kissed her breasts before, and she not only loved it, she craved it. She loved Arnold, but was afraid that because she wore leg braces he would not want her for a wife, when there were so many other women out there without her problem.

Her fears were for naught. Arnold bought an engagement ring from his cousin, Larry Levine, who was a jeweler on West

47th Street. The stone was so big it could cause permanent retina damage if observed from the wrong angle.

While seated on her well-worn gray velvet couch, he said that he had something for her. Arnold took out the ring, showed it to her, and asked "Annie Walsh, will you marry me?"

Instantly, years of rejection, humiliation, disappointment, and ridicule came to a head for her. She had always thought that she would never marry because of her handicap.

At once she was both overjoyed and choked with emotion, as she said "Of course, Arnold, I'll marry you. I love you."

Then, suddenly, a torrent of tears came flowing from her eyes as Annie hugged her fiancé, and a lifetime of loneliness, sadness, and heartbreak came pouring out of her all at once.

YOU'VE GOT TO COOL IT...

Arnold broke the news of his engagement to his partner, Wayne Harrison. Wayne had divorced his drug addict wife, and got custody of his two teenage sons. He was a man who endured a very difficult life. His whole world revolved around the job, his boys, and his Baptist church in Queens. He was a good man, but inside he was very bitter and angry about the hand that life had dealt him. He wished Arnold well, sort of, by saying "Well, I hope she's better than the bitch I married."

It was not a ringing endorsement of married life, to be sure.

At 6:30 P.M. they brought in a prisoner to the Precinct. The arrested man had gone berserk and slashed his wife in the face and torso with a machete. He cut the woman's nose off, and it was dangling by a small piece of flesh. After an initial fight, they managed to restrain and rear cuff their man after he had gone psycho at the scene.

Harrison was a very devout Christian and had a bad habit of preaching to the criminals he arrested, trying to save their souls. In this particular case, they were standing in front of the desk as Lt. Cantorwicz was booking another prisoner. Wayne started in with his sermon: "You better change your criminal ways, Mister. You're going to go straight to hell if you don't follow Jesus in your life."

Although rear cuffed, the man went into an insane rage, kicking, biting and screaming, as if he were possessed by the devil. It took four cops to bring him down.

Lt. Cantorwicz took Harrison aside and said "Wayne, you've got to cool it with the Billy Graham routine. I know you mean

196

well, but these people are just plain crazy. They're not normal, that's why they do the things that they do. They are never going to get religion, because they're too fucked up. You could have Jesus come down from the cross, and these assholes would probably rob and stab Him."

HILDA HEIDER, HARRIDAN

McInerney came to work pissed off as hell. I could tell he had a big time bug up his ass. He loved his wife, Greta, but despised her mother, Hilda Heider. He called her *Hilda Himmler*, and used to tell his friends that she was drummed out of the Gestapo........ for cruelty. Actually, Hilda came to America in 1939 and settled in Ridgewood, Queens. Back in Bavaria, she had been a member of the Hitler Jugden Korps, (Youth Corps), a distinction that Tommy loved to shove in her sour-kraut face from time to time.

Simply put, Hilda Heider and Tommy McInerney hated each other. The easygoing Tommy could not stand her constant put downs about him being a cop. Greta had once been engaged to a wealthy banker, but they broke up without marrying.

Hilda liked to bring it up to humiliate Tommy whenever she could, which was often. She was a nasty, evil harridan, with a tongue that could clip a hedge. It was a shame, because her husband, Karl, was a real nice man. He was very quiet, apparently because he could never get a word in around his shrew of a wife.

Hilda did have one positive thing going for her. At age forty-eight she still had a pair of tits that looked like the front bumper of a '57 Cadillac Eldorado, and she loved to show them off.

At Greta's urging, they went to her parents' house for dinner the night before. Everything was going well, until Hilda got her load on and began to belittle Tommy for the low pay he was getting. He tried to ignore it, until she started ridiculing him for not being man enough to support his family. A New York City cop has the normal payroll deductions for federal, state and city taxes, Social Security, and Medicare. In addition, medical insurance, union dues

198

and pension contributions were also being withheld. As far as the pension goes, the younger you are when you start, the more they take out of your check; the theory being that you are going to live longer to collect your pension, so you have to pay more into the fund.

Our take home pay was absurd for the work we were doing. We also had our pay cut by sixty dollars a week. The last thing Tommy needed was his drunken mother-in-law rubbing salt in the wound. Karl tried to calm his wife down and shut her up, to no avail. He was mortified for Tommy, and apologized over and over. Karl took his bottle of Jaegermeister out of the freezer and suggested that they have a drink of it, since it is supposed to enhance digestion.

Jaegermeister is a popular, but vile tasting German liqueur that is made from roots. Many German-American families have a bottle of it in their freezers, ready to break out at an opportune moment.

The last thing Hilda needed was more liquor. Tommy, Greta and Karl sipped their drinks, and Hilda swigged hers, like a Bowery bum drinking a bottle of Ripple. After three Jaegermeisters she was totally plastered, and meaner than ever.

She started on Tommy again. "Hey, *McIninney*, do you know where an Irish family goes on vacation? ....To a different bar."

That was Hilda's first joke for the night.

Tommy struck back "Hilda, did you hear the one about the German comedian? ....Neither did I, ...because there aren't any."

Hilda struck again. "*McIninney*, you know what a seven course Irish dinner is? .... It's a six pack of beer and a boiled potato."

Had they not had such a vitriolic relationship, the repartee would have been hilarious. After a few more ethnic insults, Tommy got up from the table and shook his father-in-law's hand and said "Good night, Karl." Then turning to his mother-in-law, he clicked his heels and said "Guten Nacht, Sie Hexe." (Good night, you witch).

I was not in a position to give advice here, since my own in-laws were terrific people. All I could do was sympathize, but not empathize.

Tommy could not stop talking about the night before. "Every fucking time I go over there I have to listen to this woman put me down. I love being a cop, and despite the low pay, I can't wait to get to work every day. So, fuck this kraut bitch! My wife is a gem, and nothing like her mother, thank Christ. But, Jimmy, I just can't go there any more."

I tried to calm my partner down. "It's family, Tommy. You just can't drop off the radar screen over a minor fight. You have to use psychology on a woman like Hilda. Look, I'm no Abigail fucking Van Buren, but the next time you're off, invite her and Karl over for dinner and treat her like a queen. I mean German appetizers, sauerbraten, red cabbage, potato pancakes, and apple sauce. Of course, some chilled bottles of Zeller Schwartze Katze to drink, and Jaegermeister for after dinner. Top it all off with a German Black Forest cake for dessert. You have that German butcher out in Maspeth; have him prepare everything. Throw your mother-in-law a curve ball. She'll have nothing to complain about, and you'll wind up smelling like a rose.

"You know, Tommy, Mary Ann and I are trying to have a baby. Maybe if you and Greta got pregnant, this problem would all go away, and your mother-in-law would be nice to you."

"Well partner", he said, "It's not for lack of trying."

SERGEANT MC NALLY RETURNS

Sgt. Kieran McNally came back to work after spending three weeks at "the farm." He was looking a bit gaunt, despite having gained a few pounds. He had not had a drink in three weeks, but he still had the ruddy, red face that cops call *the Irish sunburn*. His mother-in-law told him that if he goes off the wagon again, she would go to Family Court to take the children away from him. Although McNally had many failings, he was a loyal father to his kids, drunk or sober.

Captain Fitzgerald took Sgt. McNally into his office and let him know that there will be no 'next time.' If he starts hitting the sauce again, he'll lose the job.

I never liked McNally, and wondered how long it would be until he started drinking again. He was such a nasty drunk, and would probably be a mean dry-drunk. Tommy had the opposite opinion, and said that he would never do anything to lose his kids, or the job.

A week after coming back, McNally had desk duty and began to feel severe abdominal pains. We were in the station house having our meal break. Darlene Pignatano, the switchboard operator, screamed out loud when Sergeant McNally passed out on the floor. Cops are basically cynical by nature, and the first thing I suspected was that Lawless was drinking. However, he had no smell of alcohol on his breath, and he was sweating profusely. When he came to, he said to me and Tommy "Take me to Bellevue. I have bad stomach pains. I don't know what's wrong."

He was too large a man to carry to the radio car, so an ambulance was called. Tommy rode in the ambulance with him, and I followed in the car. The staff at Bellevue was fantastic, as always. They took McNally in and gave him a thorough examination, with x-rays and blood tests.

After an hour, a young doctor came out to see us and said "Don't say anything to the Sergeant, but I suspect that he is very ill. It may just be an inflammation of the pancreas, but due to the severe nature of the symptoms, it could be life threatening."

Tommy and I had heard of the pancreas, but didn't know what it did, or where it was. A while later, an older doctor came out and said "After reviewing the test results and the x-rays, my preliminary diagnosis is that Sergeant McNally has cancer of the pancreas and liver. There appears to be two large masses on each organ. We are going to admit him to do a biopsy. So you might as well go."

Although we were no fans of McNally, we gave him the courtesy of saying good-bye. He asked us to call his mother-in-law to tell her that he was being admitted. The veteran cop knew for months that something was not right with him, but he ignored the warning signs. He feared going to a doctor, because he did not want to find out what was causing his pains. Years of alcohol abuse had taken their toll on him. The biopsies were taken about 9:00 P.M. and it was confirmed that Kieran McNally had stage four cancer of the liver and pancreas. It was inoperable. I had no use for the man, but felt bad for his family, nevertheless.

I recalled the Cynical Proverb: "Time Wounds All Heels."

"WHAT'S THE DIFFERENCE?"

At 10:00 P.M. it was still hot in Manhattan. Tommy and I were drenched in sweat from going from one job to another. Suddenly, the dispatcher hit the alert button and blasted out a report of a kidnapping in progress in the 6th Precinct, at 7th Avenue South and Bleecker Street. The suspects were two white males, driving a white Caddy convertible, with a black top. At least one man was armed. They had forced another white male into the car at gunpoint.

I knew the 6th Precinct well, spending my first years on patrol in Greenwich Village. The West Village was a virtual rabbit warren of twisting, turning, one-way streets, some only a block long, and some hidden by an obscure wooden doorway, or iron gate. You had to work there a long time in order to learn them all. Since Bleecker Street went from west to east, I decided to head west along 14th Street to 6th Avenue, and patiently waited on 6th Avenue, near the corner of W. 17th Street.

Within less than one minute, a beat-up white Caddy convertible came roaring north on 6th Avenue, with two white trash types in the front, and another in the back seat. I knew right then and there that we had our men. After informing the dispatcher that we had the car under observation, we hit the roof lights and began pursuit. The driver was no amateur. He hit the gas and sped off up 6th Avenue, weaving in and out of traffic, with his wheels burning rubber. We were right behind him.

At 28th Street the Caddy got bogged down in traffic. With McInerney's .38 Special stuck in his ear, the driver of the getaway vehicle decided that it would be a good career move to stop the car at this point. The kidnapped man was a drug dealer who didn't pay up, so he was not a victim for whom anyone could have sympathy. After handcuffing the two suspects, a loaded .44 caliber revolver was found under the front seat.

This was a great collar. It was my turn to *catch*, so I arraigned my two prisoners in the morning.

There was a sleazy lawyer who had an office in downtown Manhattan. Her name was Hortense J. Schmucklein, a partner in the firm of Gonif, Schmucklein and Dreckmann. She was an unctuous, bottom feeding lawyer who prowled the halls of the courthouse, looking for clients. Her specialty was pimps and hookers. When criminal defendants had private attorneys their cases were heard first. The pimps would retain Schmucklein or her partners, Gary Gonif and Bruno Dreckmann, and they would plead all of the prostitutes guilty. The hookers paid a $100 fine and went home. Gonif, Schmucklein charged them $100 a head, all paid in cash.

Although she made a decent living in the Criminal Court, Schmucklein was not a good attorney. The Correction Officers and street cops called her "The Key to The Tombs" ("The Tombs" was the nickname for the Manhattan jail). Nearly all of her non-prostitute clients were found guilty and did time. Schmucklein was despised by cops because of her underhanded, dishonest way of cross-examining police witnesses. The two kidnappers were from out of town, and a family member retained Hortense J. Schmucklein, Esq. as their attorney. The lawyer put on a dog and pony show at the arraignment, mostly to impress her clients in front of the judge. The judge, having read the complaint of kidnapping and weapon possession, remanded the defendants without bail. As a concession to Schmucklein, who was now in high dudgeon, he ordered a hearing for 9:30 A.M. the next morning.

I was ready for this shyster, having gone up against her several times before. Upon taking the stand, I was sworn in as the prosecution's first and only witness. Although the Assistant D.A.

was young and not very experienced, he brought me through the direct examination like a seasoned veteran. My testimony was smooth as a baby's butt. I recounted hearing the radio call, seeing the Caddy come north on 6th Avenue, pursuing the vehicle, freeing the kidnapping victim and recovering a loaded .44 caliber revolver under the front seat.

Schmucklein was at her obnoxious best. She went through her normal routine of accusing me of planting the gun, needing glasses, not being a weapons expert, no search warrant, and so forth. And to piss me off further, she kept intentionally mispronouncing my name as 'Officer Kavendish', 'Officer Keaveney', and other variations.   After the fifth time, I said "Counselor, my name is *Kavanaugh*, not Kavendish, not Keaveney, not Keeney."

Schmucklein sneered and said "Well, well, *Mr. Kavanaugh*, a little thin skinned today, aren't you? Kavanaugh, Kavendish, Keaveney, what's the difference?"

I zeroed in. "Well, *Ms. Schmuck*, I want my name pronounced correctly!"

Having hit Hortense J's sensitivity nerve dead on, she reflexively said "My name is *Schmucklein*, not *Schmuck*! .... Do you understand that, Officer *Kavanaugh*?"

With the glint of a smile, I responded "Schmuck, Schmucklein....... what's the difference?"

The judge was no admirer of the attorney and had to cover his face, because he was laughing so hard. Schmucklein was enraged, and the veins in her neck were ready to burst. In an angry outburst she screamed at me: "Officer Kavanaugh, are you trying to show contempt for me?"

Remembering a line from the old W.C. Fields and Mae West movie, *My Little Chickadee,* I said "No, madam, I'm doing my best to hide it."

Both defendants were remanded to The Tombs, without bail, and would be indicted within a week by the Grand Jury.

A CHARACTER FROM THE PAST

We received a notice in the department mail that the civilian complaint lodged against us by Wellington Hartshorne was closed out as "unsubstantiated." Even though the complainant admitted that he lied, the NYPD did not like to have a finding of "unfounded." The desk jockeys at the C.C.R.B. have an "eat your own" mentality which adversely affects the morale of the patrol cops. "Unsubstantiated" means that the event may have happened, but there was not enough proof against the cop. "Unfounded" means that it just did not happen. Anyway, I was happy to put that one behind me.

The Sunday day shift is usually the quietest one for cops. However, at about 3:20 P.M. we got a call to handle a fight at the Hotel Seville on East 29th Street and Madison Avenue. The Seville was once a nice, clean, respectable hotel, with a marble lobby, but it had seen better days. There were a lot of welfare tenants and drug addicts in the place now. The Seville was desperately trying to hang on by showing a veneer of respectability, but it had about as much effect as spraying perfume on a pile of shit.

Even so, the call to investigate a fight on the ninth floor of the Seville on a Sunday afternoon struck me as odd. We knocked on the door to room 907, and a haggard, gray haired, whiskey-breathed woman in a red dress answered the door and let us in. Inside the hotel room there was another old hag, and a tall, distinguished looking man in his early sixties, dressed in a rumpled blue sport jacket, white shirt, and gray tie. His head of silver hair needed a trim, and he hadn't shaved in a few days, but the man still had a quiet aura of dignity and grace about him. The three of them had been drinking all afternoon and were well in their cups. The entire room reeked of cheap scotch. The women had engaged in a drunken cat fight, and a neighbor called the police.

I took a look at the old man again and thought that there was something very familiar about him, but I just could not recall ever meeting him. Tommy had a short fuse, and one of the women quickly got under his skin. Forgetting that Madison Avenue was one of the places where he was not supposed to speak, McInerney said to one of the boozed up women "Don't light any matches in here, lady. The breath from you three bozos will blow the place up."

With that, one of the women got indignant and said "How dare you speak like that to Captain Video!"

Upon hearing the woman's remark, I took a closer look at the man who was now standing about five feet from me, and tried to imagine him twenty or twenty-five years younger. I quickly realized that the old man was Al Hodge who played the role of Captain Video on the old Dumont Television Network from 1951 to 1955. It was a great show, and it was named "Captain Video and His Video Rangers."

After the show folded in 1955, Hodge did not lack for work, becoming a writer and producer. However, by 1975, after a failed marriage, he had fallen into chronic alcoholism and wound up in a $90 a week hotel room in Manhattan. Ironically, you could see his old studio at Rockefeller Center from his room at the Seville.

I approached the man with a sense of great admiration and awe, and introduced myself. After all, I had been one of the Captain's Video Rangers.

"Mr. Hodge, it's an honor to meet you. I was a great fan of your show, and I was a Video Ranger, too." And that was no blarney.

The elderly man's sad eyes lit up and he broke out in a huge smile. He had accomplished many things in life: actor, writer, television producer, and U.S. Navy officer during World War II, but he would always be remembered as "Captain Video." Mr.

Hodge was genuinely thrilled to meet one of his Video Rangers whom he had entertained a generation ago, during the Golden Age of Television.

Curiously, I asked: "Mr. Hodge, whatever happened to your young sidekick, Don Hastings? He was one of my favorite characters on the show."

The Captain replied "Well, Jimmy, the last I heard, Don went on to become a famous soap opera star. He is living somewhere in California. We used to keep in touch, but I haven't heard from him in a long time."

Tommy never saw the show, so he had no idea what we were talking about, until I explained who Captain Video was. Hodge poured drinks for us. Although I hated scotch, there was no way I was turning this drink down.

We sat on the couch looking at his huge Captain Video scrapbook. After half an hour or so, realizing that it was time to finish up the tour, I said "Well, Captain, it's time to say good-bye. It was really great to meet you, Mr. Hodge. Until we, and your Video Rangers, meet again!"

"Thanks for stopping by, boys" said a beaming Captain Video, as he patted me on the back, like I was his favorite nephew.

For the time being, old Al Hodge made me feel like I was the most important man in the world. It was a great feeling for a guy like me who was beaten down in life, and dead broke. Well, we both had something in common.

I got an autographed photo of Captain Video in full uniform, and one of the evil Dr. Pauli. It hurt me greatly to see one of my boyhood heroes slowly drinking himself to death. Sadly, I would never see my beloved Captain Video again.

One of the hardest lessons in life is learning that some of your childhood heros have clay feet.

THE QUIET MAN HAS A PROBLEM

Sean Dennihy, the man from Highway Patrol One, had no steady partner. Dennihy was from the northeast Bronx, 45th Pct., and I was from the opposite end of the city, the 123rd Pct., in the southwest part of Staten Island. We lived about forty miles or more from each other, but had lived parallel lives: Irish-German family, married, U.S. Army veterans, and Catholic grade and high school alumni. Sean looked upon me as a kindred spirit, and a man he could trust. The feeling was mutual. He didn't talk much, and kept mostly to himself; thus his nickname in the Precinct was "The Quiet Man."

Dennihy had a personal problem and saw me as a man he could confide in. After one day shift, Sean asked if we could go to Rolf's to discuss something personal. Between 4:00 and 4:30 P.M. Rolf's was usually pretty quiet, then its steady bar crowd came in. Henry the bartender greeted us : "Beers for you boys, Jimmy?"

"You got it, Henry. I'm so dry, I'm fartin' dust."

I was so dehydrated from the day's heat and humidity that my tongue soaked up the first Lowenbrau draft, and it never even hit my stomach.

Dennihy got right to the point. "Jimmy, what I am about to tell you is very personal and must be kept confidential. I know that you and your *son,* Tommy McInerney, are very tight, but this has to be kept close to the vest."

"Sean, you know that anything you tell me will remain a secret forever, right to my fucking grave."

"I appreciate that, Jimmy, that's why I am going to confide in you.

"My wife Bridget and I have been married for five years. She is a nurse at Albert Einstein Medical Center in the Bronx. We have no kids, and never really had a good sex life. I attributed it to her rigid Catholic upbringing, but I loved her, and accepted it. Since I came to the 13th, she has been acting very strangely. She doesn't speak much lately, and has turned nasty as hell. I'm not a wife beater, swordsman, gambler, or drunk, so I didn't know what the problem was. I suspected that she was getting screwed by someone at work. You know, Jimmy, I could accept that and just ask her for a divorce, but what I am about to tell you must remain absolutely confidential."

"Of course, Sean. It goes without saying."

"The other night Bridget said she was going out with some friends. So, I followed her to this house on Mayflower Avenue. A woman got in her car and they took off. I tailed them to a restaurant in midtown Manhattan. They stayed for two hours.

When Bridget and her friend left, they drove back to the Bronx, and parked about half a block from the woman's Mayflower Avenue house. Next fucking thing you know, they're making out in the front seat. Then, the other woman took Bridget into the back seat, and ....I...... couldn't believe what the fuck I saw."

I felt badly for the man, and said "I get the picture, Sean."

"You know, Jimmy, I was prepared for just about anything, but this. My wife in love with another woman! What the fuck is that all about? I checked the broad out, and she is a doctor at Albert Einstein Medical Center, and married to a plastic surgeon. Her name is Dr. Elise Goldfarb."

I felt a gut-wrenching angst for my friend, but really didn't know what to say to him. During my tenure in the 6th Precinct in the West Village, I got to know a lot of gay men and women, and liked most of them.

"You know, Sean, before I came here, I worked in the Village for many years. Prior to that time, I didn't know any gays. I soon found out that they are just like everyone else, except by virtue of their hormones, or whatever, they are attracted to the same sex. They are bankers, lawyers, cops, firemen, secretaries, nurses, doctors, plumbers, clergy, and everything else. So, you can't think of them any less than you would a person who was left handed.

"Now, in Bridget's case, she probably knew since puberty that she was gay, or maybe AC-DC. Don't you think that this poor woman was tormented about being gay in a straight world, and tried to fake it for her family's sake?

"I'm sure that she really does love you, but due to circumstances beyond her control, she is more attracted to women than men. Don't ask Bridget to be someone she isn't. It's not fair to her, Sean."

"Christ, Jimmy! That's easy for you to say. This is the fucking woman I chose to marry!"

"Look, Sean, any time you have someone in an embarrassing situation, always give them a graceful way out to save face. It's the same as on the job. You get some 140 pound "Three Beer Sampson" who wants to take on everyone in the bar, then he realizes he is going to get his ass kicked. You get him on the side and tell him that he really does not want to hurt everyone in the bar and get locked up. Then you ask him, as a personal favor to you, if he will leave peacefully and not hurt anyone. They guy will usually agree to go, having been given a graceful way out, saying that he really wasn't scared, but was just helping out the cop. But, above all, always be prepared for the guy's sucker punch.

"What I would recommend is that you do your homework first. Go to the hospital and identify yourself as a cop to the security guards, but don't give your name. They are probably retired cops. Ask them for the real scoop about Dr. Goldfarb, and see what type of person she is. Then we'll meet back here to discuss what you found out."

DENNIHY REPORTS BACK

Three days later Sean and I were back at Rolf's. Dennihy told me that, just as I predicted, the security guards knew what was going on. Sean said "They told me that Dr. Elise Goldfarb was a switch-hitter, who was married to the famous plastic surgeon, Dr. Merton Goldfarb. She had screwed her former husband out of a fortune, and was one very vindictive, money grubbing bitch. She was now having a hot and heavy affair with one of the nurses, Bridget Dennihy. It killed me to hear that from a stranger."

"Well, Sean, women can be vicious and vindictive at times, so I recommend that you hire a private eye to follow her and get some photos of her and Goldfarb, just for insurance. Then, without showing her the photos, approach her and say that since you have not been getting along, you would like to separate. If she is O.K. with her relationship with Dr. Goldfarb, she will agree. However, if she has been listening to some feminist bitch on how to screw a husband out of his money, all bets are off. Then you have to call in your 'ace in the hole' so to speak, your photographs, to avoid the sucker-punch.

"Sean, the worst enemies in a man's marriage are his wife's sisters or girlfriends who have had marital problems. If a guy's wife listens to even one disgruntled cunt, she will poison the wife's mind, and ruin their marriage."

CONFRONTATION
WITH A WANNABEE

Staten Island experienced a population boom once the Verrazano Bridge connected the island to Brooklyn in 1964. A large contingent of Brooklynites moved there to escape their crowded neighborhoods. Among the people who came were Italian gangsters and their amateur imitators, called "wannabees" or "Guidos."

Besides moonlighting for the exterminator, I was still working for Callahan the lawyer, but not loving it. I was serving his legal papers on various defendants for over a month. Jerry did mostly personal injury, commercial litigation, and divorce work. So far, after the initial close call, I did not have a hard time. Most of the people knew the suit was coming, and just took the papers without complaint.

This hot, humid, summer evening I knew that the service would be difficult. Why else would Callahan tag along to supervise? I carried my Smith & Wesson .38 caliber Chief Special tucked deep in my waistband, and wore my shirt outside my pants to hide it. That night the target for service was a wannabee named Aldo Consellatore. He had cheated his business partner in a pizza store out of more than $300,000.00 and refused to pay it back. Consellatore threatened to kill his partner, and then Callahan got involved.

On the way there Callahan said "I don't think our boy is connected, he's just some guinea wannabee. He may try some crap, however, so be careful."

The big red Caddy pulled up in front of Consellatore's mansion in the Prince's Bay section of Staten Island. The house was adjacent

213

to Lemon Creek, a brackish stream that flowed south into tranquil Raritan Bay, and housed the mosquito capital of the northeast. There were tall, white columns in the front, a Madonna on the half-shell on the lawn, and a grotesque fountain with four cherubs spouting water from their mouths.

I got out of the car, strode up the long walkway, and rang the bell. Jerry had given me a photo of the subject so I would know if I had the right person.

A man in his mid-forties answered the door. He looked like a cartoon figure of a gangster: Black hair combed straight back, wife beater shirt, cigar in the mouth, chest and back hair that looked like a mohair sweater, Gucci loafers with no socks, and a few days growth of beard. He smelled as if he had marinated himself in Jovan Musk. This was the guy, all right.

His greeting to me was "What the fuck do you want?"

"Are you Aldo Consellatore?"

"Who the fuck wants to know?"

"I do, sir. I have some legal papers to serve on you."

"Go fuck yourself, you donkey cocksucker. Get off my property, now!"

As I was handing the legal papers to Consellatore, his ten year old son came to the door. He looked like a younger, smaller version of the father, with the same wise-guy attitude. The kid also had his chin stuck out and said "You heard the man. Get the fuck out of here now."

With that, the junior Guido hauled off to punch me with right in the balls. By the time I realized that I was about to be struck in the nuts, all I could do was move to the side a bit. The kid's punch hit my Smith & Wesson revolver dead on, breaking his hand. The little mini-gangster was crying, holding his hand and screaming in pain.

Consellatore screamed out at me as I left "You broke my kid's hand, you son of a bitch. I'll fucking kill you, you Irish bastard! You're a dead man, you fucking donkey, a fucking dead man! You hear me? Do you fuckin' hear me? Do you know who the fuck I am? I'm Aldo fucking Consellatore!"

I hurried back to the perceived safety of Callahan's Cadillac, looking over my shoulder a few times to see if I was going to get shot. After getting in the car, I said to Callahan as he peeled out, leaving ten yards of rubber, "Jerry, I don't mind serving white trash, Ricans, yoms, geeps, cocoanuts, Heebs, Polacks, donkeys, krauts, squareheads, and normal guineas, but this is the last fucking Guido I am ever going to serve for you!"

Callahan gave me an extra $20.00 for hazardous duty pay.

"...SHE SURE AS HELL AIN'T BOBBING FOR APPLES..."

Sure enough, Bridget Dennihy's mind had been poisoned by Dr. Goldfarb, one truly disgruntled bitch. Mrs. Dennihy had morphed from a nice, pleasant wife, into a money grubbing feminist. The Mayflower Avenue house where Bridget and her lover met was owned by Elise Goldfarb. She had screwed her last husband out of it, and Goldfarb and her current spouse used it sometimes when they had to be on call and near the hospital. Their main residence was in Scarsdale, a wealthy suburb north of the Bronx.

When Sean returned home about 5:00 P.M., Bridget was ready to pounce on him, like a cat on a mouse. She told him that he was a terrible man, a bad husband, and she wanted a divorce. In addition, she wanted all of the bank accounts, and the house. Sean anticipated the request for a divorce, but he was floored by the vindictive nature of Bridget's demands, and her vicious manner. This was not like her at all.

Sean could barely speak. When he finally could, he said "What did I do to you that would make you want to hurt me like this?"

She continued with her act. "I just can't stand living with you any longer. You have to get out of here for my mental health."

It was a ration of crap, right of the feminist handbook.

Dennihy tried to reason with her. "Bridget, I haven't done anything to you to deserve this treatment, and you know it. If you want a divorce, there is no problem, but let's split everything, fifty-fifty."

Bridget was spitting fire. "No, Sean, I want it all, and I want you out of here right now! All I have to do is make one phone call

216

to Internal Affairs and say that you have beaten me several times, and threatened me with your gun. I know how to play the game and screw you up real good."

Sean stood there for a moment, having trouble believing that his kind but frigid wife had turned into this venomous barracuda. Now he was ready to drop the bomb on Bridget.

Sean said "I know that you have not been a faithful wife, Bridget. For a while I suspected that you were having an affair with someone at work......... and I was right. You are involved with that AC-DC doctor, Elise Goldfarb."

Bridget was stunned and speechless for a moment. She had been on offense, and now she was on defense. Bridget regained her composure, thinking that her husband was bluffing, and said "Are you listening to rumors started by my co-workers?"

"No, Bridget, actually I was looking at photos of you and your muff-munching doctor friend in bed together, buck naked. From what I can see, she sure as hell ain't bobbing for apples between your legs, honey", as he threw her a stack of two dozen sexually explicit photos of Bridget and Elise. Sean's wife looked like the deer in the headlights, or more like the deer that just got hit by a car. She felt like she was going to vomit. Bridget had been put up to this charade by her girlfriend, and it backfired, big time. Now, her whole world was turned upside down.

Sean, now having got his balls back, told his wife "Now, I want you out of this house, I want the deed signed over to me, as well as the bank accounts. You can do whatever the fuck you want to do after that. If you don't like it, your family will see every one of these goddamn pictures of you and your lover. Don't worry, I have several copies, plus the negatives. Bridget, you're a miserable, dishonest bitch!"

Bridget was mortified for acting the way she did and wanted to apologize to Sean, but she could not express herself correctly. It was over between them forever, and there was no going back. She made her bed, and now had to lay in it, no pun intended.

Sean was grateful to me for my advice. The money he paid to the private eye was worth every penny. He was not a mean man, but his wife's extortion plan made him play the reverse role of extortionist, in self defense.

Even though Sean had been treated cruelly and unfairly by his wife, he was such a decent man that he eventually split their assets equally, and they went their separate ways. He also burned the pictures and the negatives.

I realized that my friend from the Bronx was a better man than myself. Indeed, Sean Dennihy, The Quiet Man, was a very good and decent soul.

SHALOM, UNCLE CARL

It was a typical summer night on the midnight shift. Lt. Cantorwicz was the desk officer, and Winnie was the switchboard operator. On his way to work, Carl had stopped at Vincent's, in Little Italy, and picked up an order of shrimp, smothered in their famous hot sauce. About 2:00 A.M., Elvis was serenading the staff in front of the desk, and was hardly noticed by anyone as he sung his heart out with a lame, highly forgettable rendition of *Heartbreak Hotel*. His talent escaped everyone within earshot.

The weird couple from the single room occupancy hotel up the block came in, and the wife, as always, had a plastic jar filled with freshly caught bedbugs, all the while complaining to the Lieutenant about the conditions in their room. Carl blew cigar smoke at them, but they blabbered on anyway.

A few moments later, Lt. Cantorwicz went to the refrigerator, retrieved his shrimp dinner, and began to eat it. About half way through his meal, he stood up, grabbed his chest, and fell to the floor. Carl's three hundred pound body made a sickening thud on the floor when it hit. His face was ashen white, and his lips were blue. NYPD Lieutenant Carl Cantorwicz, age fifty-nine, was dead of a massive heart attack before he even hit the floor.

Winnie screamed for help, but the cops in the Precinct could not revive him. We arrived in minutes, but Uncle Carl was gone, and we could do nothing for him. I was heartbroken, trying unsuccessfully to hold back tears, and crying like a baby in front of the desk, feeling like a young kid who had just lost his favorite uncle.

Life just isn't fair. Carl was one of the greatest guys I ever met, and he was taken from us in an instant. His funeral in Brooklyn would be one of the saddest days of my life. *Shalom*, I said, to my dear uncle Carl.

HEIDER, HEIDER, HEIDER, HO!!

At my suggestion, the McInerneys were hosting the Heiders for dinner. Tommy and Greta had everything ready. For appetizers, they had shrimp wrapped in bacon. The main course was sauerbraten, with potato pancakes, red cabbage and apple sauce. Greta also made green beans with *spaetzle* (German noodles).

As soon as the guests came in, Tommy greeted them. He shook Karl's hand warmly, and Hilda pecked him on the cheek, much like getting kissed by a duck.

Hilda had on a low cut blouse, which revealed her magnificent mammaries, Tommy felt guilty leering at his mother-in-law's breasts, thinking that it was some sort of latent incest, or a least a venial sin to lust after them, even though he despised her. But, tits were tits, he rationalized, regardless of the owner.

The shrimp were delicious. For wine they had Zeller Schwartze Katze, a favorite of German-Americans. After some small talk, the appetizers were finished, and they proceeded to the main course. The German butcher in Maspeth had done it up right. The sauerbraten was excellent. Greta made the potato pancakes to perfection, and the Bavarian Beans with spaetzle dish was great.

Hilda was well-behaved that evening, never once bringing up Greta's former fiancé, or Tommy's low pay. Karl was so at ease that he spoke for a change, whenever Hilda shut up. After dinner, Greta poured chilled Jaegermeister, and served Black Forest cake. McInerney turned down the Jaegermeister, and made himself a Black Forest coffee. It was like Irish coffee, but instead of Irish whiskey, he used Kirschwasser, a German cherry liqueur.

Based upon past experiences with his mother-in-law, Tommy

still waited for the true Hilda to emerge. However, just as I had advised, she had nothing to complain about. When they left about 10:00 P.M., Greta thanked Tommy for inviting them over. She was very grateful that things had gone so well.

In bed that evening, Greta had become the aggressor, nearly raping McInerney. Tommy thought that maybe it would be a good idea to have the in-laws over every week, no matter what it cost.

"WHAT YOU'VE GOT
IS ALCOHOLIC GOUT"

Coming home one early September afternoon, I was met at the door by my wife, Mary Ann, who was in tears. She had just received a call from her brother, Mike, that their mother died of a stroke in a hospital in Hazleton, PA.

Most men would secretly delight in hearing that their mother-in-law died, but not me. Helen Pavalovich treated me like she was my own mother, and I loved her a great deal. I tried to console Mary Ann for the moment, but could not. All I could do was hold her. When she regained her composure, we drove off to the small town of Freeland, in the Pocono Mountains of Pennsylvania.

The funeral in St. Mary's Byzantine Catholic church was quite different from what I was used to. Although the Byzantine Church came back under the Roman church and the pope circa 1950, they still maintained many of their old customs and ceremonies. It was like a hybrid of Roman Catholic and Greek Orthodox churches. The church rooftop exhibited two magnificent gold cupolas, and the interior was decorated in vivid red, green and gold colors. The mass was said in old Slavonic.

After the funeral, the family had a great send-off for Helen at the deceased's house. Mary Ann's brothers, cousins, and uncles were prolific drinkers. I thought that my Irish and German relatives could put the beer away, but there were mere amateurs compared to the Slovak men. These guys were professionals, who actually drank themselves sober. We feasted on kielbasa, pierogie, stuffed cabbage, and other Czech foods.

I tried to keep up with my in-laws, but passed out on the

223

couch. Waking up two hours later, they were still going, full speed. After two or three more beers, I excused myself and went to bed. At six o'clock in the morning, I woke up with a severe pain in the big toe of my right foot. The joint was beet red and throbbing. It felt like there was a red-hot ice pick in the joint. My wife thought that maybe I got up during the night and banged my toe, but I didn't remember anything like that happening.

Mary Ann called a foot doctor in Hazleton, and we made the easy seven mile trip up the mountain. Dr. Yadsko examined me and asked if I had any alcoholic beverages within the last twenty-four hours. I explained to the doctor that my mother-in-law died, and I overdid it at the post funeral party, having a dozen beers, or more. The elderly man looked at me and said "Son, what you have is alcoholic gout. It is caused by too much uric acid in the blood. The acid becomes crystalline and settles in a joint, usually the big toe, or the elbow."

Taking a syringe, the doctor drew fluid from my toe joint, which offered some relief. He showed it to me under the microscope. It looked like small crystals, with jagged edges. He said "That's what is causing your pain. Stop drinking beer for a while, and drink at least four quarts of water a day to dilute the acid and flush it out. Your kidneys were just too overwhelmed by your drinking binge to handle the shock. And take these pills for a week."

With a wink he said, "Don't try keeping up with your in-laws, son; their bodies are used to it."

FREDDIE GETS SECOND GRADE

The events of the summer of 1975 have shown Detective 3rd Grade Freddie Zarullo in a very positive light. The burglary collar was routine enough, but the armed robbery and homicide of the store manager, the murder in Union Square, the rescue of two kidnapping victims, with a homicide collar, to boot, and clearing all of the open commercial burglaries caught the eye of the Chief of Detectives. Couple this with the fact that Freddie's *rabbi* was his friend, Lt. Enzo Caruso, the aide to the Chief of Detectives, and a compelling case could be made for his promotion to Second Grade Detective, at least on paper.

On the negative side were Freddie's annual evaluation reports by his immediate supervisor, Sgt. Herring. They were unflattering, at best, sprinkled with adjectives like "lethargic' and "unmotivated", with great lines like "coasting toward retirement in neutral gear, on an empty gas tank." Another said "He brings the word *sloth* down to a new level." Stealing a line from Winston Churchill, Herring wrote "An empty Plymouth Fury pulled up to the 13th Pct., and Detective Zarullo got out."

Normally, a detective with those evaluations would be transferred or demoted. However, political forces in the department kept Freddie entrenched. The Detective Squad commander, Lt. Van Ostrand, was a hands-off boss. He would come in, look at all the incoming cases, confer with Sgt. Herring and the detectives about the current files, then head off to Molly Malone's for a martini. Basically, Sgt. Herring ran the show.

Lt. Caruso tried to convince the Chief of Detectives that the reason for Freddie's poor evaluations was a personality clash between

Sgt. Herring and Zarullo. The Chief was a little skeptical, and called Sgt. Herring for his input. After listening to the Sergeant, he learned that two of Freddie's homicide cases were actually broken by a 13th Pct. uniformed cop named Arnold Levine, who got dumped back to patrol from his long time position in the Lab. The Union Square murder case was handed to him on a silver platter by another uniformed cop, in the Anawanda Club bar after work.

Herring knew how Freddie solved the west side burglaries, with one cut of his knife, but, even given the animosity between the two, no cop would ever rat out another cop for something like this, especially when a worthless criminal got what was coming to him.

The Chief did not want to hurt his loyal aide, Lt. Caruso, by denying Zarullo's promotion. Next, he pulled Arnold's personnel file and carefully reviewed it. The file contained glowing letters of congratulation from District Attorneys, former Chiefs of Detectives, Borough Commanders, and Police Commissioners for the outstanding work Levine had done on various cases over the past fifteen years. There were some negative evaluations that the Chief saw, but he recognized the bosses as nasty, petty men, who probably saw Arnold as a threat to their jobs.

After finishing his review of the file, he wondered why Arnold Levine was not promoted to Detective a decade before. He had qualified for promotion many times over. On top of this, in just two months on patrol, Levine had earned two Meritorious Police Duty awards, and two Commendations. To correct this injustice, Chief of Detectives Alvin Gartenstein decided to promote Arnold Levine to Third Grade Detective. Reluctantly, he also promoted Freddie Zarullo to Second Grade Detective.

A Second Grade detective made Sergeant's pay. Upon hearing of Freddie's promotion, Sgt. Herring immediately went to the Manhattan South Detective headquarters and asked for a transfer. There was no way he could work with Freddie as a Second Grade detective, making the same pay as him.

PARTY AT THE ANAWADA

The Friday after Labor Day, Zarullo made Second Grade, and Arnold Third Grade Detective. For Levine, it was totally unexpected. In June, he was a 150 lb. milquetoast pencil pusher in the Police Lab, and in September, he was a 150 lb. decorated street cop, with a chest full of well-earned medals.

The notification from Lt. von Richter the day before to report to Police H.Q. at 9:00 A.M. the next day hit Levine right out of the blue. Freddie Z. had over twenty seven years on the job and knew how to play the politics of the department. But for the naïve Levine, this was a dream come true. With "Wonder Woman" at his side, he had his picture taken with the Police Commissioner and Chief of Detectives Gartenstein.

Freddie had coveted Second Grade for years, and he held a lavish party at the Anawanda Club. McSorley and his son did it up right. Freddie got Arnold to split the tab, even though most of the guests were friends of Zarullo.

BREAKING THE ICE

Little did Arnold know, but his estranged parents had been secretly tracking his new career as a patrol cop in the daily papers. His name and photo had been in the Daily News and the Post many times that summer, and the story of his promotion was even in the New York Times.

Arnold and his parents had not spoken in fifteen years. He loved his parents, but they had been unreasonably vindictive and hostile to him over the half-assed arranged marriage they tried to rope him into. So, he shut them out of his life, and vice-versa. Sadly, his parents, Melvin and Sarah, only lived about three blocks away from Arnold in Brooklyn, and he was their only child.

The phone rang in Arnold Levine's apartment about 7:00 P.M. Upon answering, a man's voice said "Is that you, Arnold?"

"Yes, who is this?"

"It's your father. How are you? I read in the Times that they promoted you to Detective. Congratulations."

After fifteen years of not speaking to his parents, Arnold didn't know what to say. The only words he could muster were "Thanks, Dad, so what's new with you and mom?"

"Nothing; how about you?"

"Well, I just got engaged to a wonderful girl and we are getting married soon."

"She's Jewish, right?"

"No, dad! We've been down this road before, remember? She's an Irish Catholic woman, and I love her to death, and she loves me, O.K.?"

"All right, already, I'm not complaining. She could be a

228

schwartze for all I care. I'm happy for you, son. When are you getting married?"

"Probably in one week or so. Do you and mom want to come?"

"Does Sabbath come on Friday night? Of course, we'll come."

Sarah Levine was listening in the background and ascertained that Arnold was getting married. She was overjoyed, and too emotional to speak to her son.

A CLOSE CALL

With Tommy taking the day off for some personal business, I was working with Aloysius Jackson for the night. You could not want for a better partner than Al. He was a proud, confident man, but not arrogant. Al lived in Springfield Gardens, Queens, with his wife and three daughters. I had worked with Jackson for a few days in July and he had given me a lesson in real police work, when we served warrants together.

Although New York City was in the financial shit-hole, there was a lot of construction going on in the neighborhood: apartment houses, senior citizen centers, schools, etc. There was a group of black agitators who tried to coerce and extort no-show jobs from the various contractors at the construction sites, in the name of "civil rights."

They would threaten to picket the job site, claiming racial discrimination, if they did not get the fictitious jobs. Once they were successful, they would provide the manager with two or more phony names and Social Security numbers, and pick up the checks every payday. It was the cost of doing business for racial peace in New York, and, it was the ultimate perversion of the civil rights movement in America. A once noble and righteous cause had deteriorated into a cheap shakedown racket.

At 6:45 A.M. we received a tip from the foreman on a construction site on East 29th Street, between First and Second Avenues, that the Black United Reparations Project was going to launch a full scale attack on his project sometime after 7:00 A.M., either today or tomorrow. One of his black workers heard

230

something in a bar where he hung out, and it sounded credible.

There was nothing out of the ordinary that morning, so, around 7:15, we got our coffee and decided to hang out near the job site for a while. As we started sipping our drinks, four large vehicles, the size of laundry trucks, came whipping around the corner from First Avenue and stopped right in front of the construction site.

On a prearranged signal, about twenty men came out of each truck, brandishing electrical conduit, pipes, chains, and other weapons. All that Jackson could do was grab the radio mike and shout frantically into the radio "10-13, two-nine, First to Second!"

We got out of the car to do battle, but the odds were overwhelming. Not expecting much help from Logan and his crew, we figured out that we were going to get a severe beating or even killed. There was a hard core of about fifteen men who were assigned just to beat us into submission. Then the others would then attack the workers.

All we could do was to take cover behind a three foot pile of bricks and construction debris. We had guns drawn, in the combat crouch, and ready to shoot anyone who brandished a weapon against us. Our adversaries could see in our eyes that we were not bluffing, and they kept a few feet away. The Mexican standoff lasted for several seconds, when the loud mouth leader said from the rear of the crowd "Go on, go get the cops! They can't kill all of us."

Mr. Loudmouth was correct—but at least we would take down twelve of them. As the crowd of pipe swinging men came closer, my sweaty index finger was caressing the trigger of my .38 caliber Smith and Wesson six shot revolver. It was now about 7:20 A.M., and although Logan and the Moon Dogs had gotten a little better, it was too close to quitting time for them to show up, I thought.

It was the most scared I had been since that day at the Elton Hotel when the psycho pulled the knife on me and Tommy. Because of my extreme fright, I did not even hear the sound of sirens coming up First Avenue, and radio cars coming the wrong way down East 29th Street.

My right index finger tugged on the trigger, ready to fire, as I sized up the closest man to me who was swinging a long metal pipe close to my head. He was getting closer and closer, and Al and I had nowhere to go. This pipe-swinging fool was going to take one square in his chest in about two seconds.

Having been preoccupied with trying to save our own lives, I now began to see Logan and his boys coming into the battle. They saw our plight and came at our attackers from the rear, cracking skulls and kicking ass, with a brutal nightstick and blackjack assault. They mowed down the agitators like a farmer with a scythe. It looked like a battlefield, with bleeding, battered bodies lying all over the street.

I holstered my weapon and immediately vaulted over the pile of bricks and went right at the man who was trying to hit me in the head with the pipe. I must have looked like a lunatic, because the guy got all bug-eyed, but he still held up his pipe and swung it at my head again. I parried the blow and hit him in the arm. My bayonet training in the army paid off. My attacker did not know how to use his weapon by parrying his opponent's moves and then thrusting. However, he was a worthy adversary and the two of us were dueling in the middle of the street like pirates. With one last thrust I hit him in the solar plexus twice, backed up with my full body weight, causing him to drop the pipe and collapse into the fetal position on the street, holding his stomach.

Al and I then went into the building to help the construction workers. It turned out that they did not need any assistance. They were primed, armed, and ready, and they delivered a world class ass- kicking to this pack of shakedown artists. This was one construction site that would not be making any payoffs.

Danny Della Donna was in the thick of the fray. Danny was about fifty years old, and was a tremendous physical specimen. He was picking men up and throwing them around, while Sgt. Byrne turned one guy into a human piñata.

Those attackers who could still move ran for their trucks and sped off. The others were collared for riot, assault, weapons

232

possession and resisting arrest.

Back at the station house, Jackson took the collars because he needed the overtime. I met up with Logan and his group of Long Islanders in the locker room and thanked them for saving our asses.

Just several weeks before, we would have been severely beaten or even killed. But now there was a new atmosphere in the command. It was a real brotherhood of men doing a dangerous job, needing each other for protection, and always being there for the other guy. It was the way it should be, and would be from now on, in Manhattan South's 13th Precinct.

MEETING FATHER CHARLIE

After nearly four years of marriage, Mary Ann and I had no children, and assumed that we just could not have any. Arriving home in the late morning after the battle at the construction site, I fell into a deep, dreamless sleep and awoke about 5:00 P.M. when my wife came home from work.

I noticed that Mary Ann was beaming, looking like she won the lottery. "Jimmy, I have good news. I'm pregnant. The doctor is concerned about the position of the baby, and he told me not to work until after the baby is born. "

It was the last thing I expected her to say. I was so choked up that I couldn't even speak, and just hugged my wife for a long time. I wanted to be a father, and knew in my heart that I would be a better parent than my own father, a very flawed man. I also didn't care if my wife worked. Somehow, we would make it work without her salary.

The events of the past several months since returning to patrol have caused me to reassess my life. I was never so broke, now working three jobs, unable to put gas in my car, barely making my mortgage payment, and had to cash my paycheck in a bar. The addict nearly shooting me with my own gun was a real epiphany. Then, there was the Elton Hotel *clusterfick* – nearly getting indicted—the man burned alive, Ben's illness, the inability to help my brother Frank, the Pennsylvania kid who was killed, Uncle Carl's death, the (now) one armed butcher boy, the close call in the subway, and everything else that transpired on patrol this summer. I was emotionally shell-shocked, and financially busted, but for some reason I was having a lot of laughs every day at work. Maybe it was just to keep from crying.

The heavy work load and the constant dealing with heartbreak, sorrow, death and violence had caused me to become a jaded, hardened, and insensitive man. So much so, that I had virtually put religion and God out of my life. Two days later it was Sunday, and I decided to walk around the corner to the local church to attend 8:00 A.M. mass. I had not been there for a few years, and sat in the last pew.

The priest was a man in his mid-forties, with a pleasant Irish brogue and a fine wit. He had a knack for telling a story, as most Irishmen do. His sermon was about forgiving family members and others who may have hurt you along life's way.

"The grudge holder is the one who always loses" was Father Charles Higgins' lesson for the day.

At the end of mass I stayed to say a prayer for my unborn child and my wife. Upon leaving church, the priest was waiting by the front door and greeted me warmly. "Top of the marnin' to ye', sir! I haven't seen ye' here before. I'm Father Charles Higgins, comin' to ye' by way of County Cork. And who is it I may have the pleasure of speakin' ta, this foine marnin?"

I looked at the priest sheepishly and said "Well, Father, actually I grew up here, but I haven't been back for some time. The name's Jimmy Kavanaugh."

"Well, with a name like Kavanaugh we're off to a good start. So, Jimmy, what brings ye' back home?"

"I'm a cop in Manhattan, Father, and I see some of the worst things in life. After all these years, I have just become so hardened and cynical that I don't think I believe in God any more. My wife is pregnant, and I want to believe, but then I sometimes feel that it's all nonsense. Basically, Father Higgins, I've lost my faith."

"Well, Jimmy, God hasn't given up on you, although sometimes you may think He has. We'll talk again, and don't be a stranger. You know, I became a priest later in life. I was a musician with an Irish band, and I toured all over the world, playing the concertina in

235

America, Australia, and all of Europe. One day I realized that my calling was not music, but the priesthood, and here I am. Don't forget, Jimmy, that you can be away from the church for a while, but when you want to come back, the church will always be here for you."

I took an instant liking to this man and said "Thanks for talking to me, Father Higgins. I want you to know that I'm not some born-again Christian looking to find Jesus."

"Oh, don't worry, Kavanaugh, He was never lost......... you were! And, please, just call me *Father Charlie* from now on."

WEDDING BELLS ARE RINGING

Not believing in long engagements, Arnold Levine and Annie Walsh agreed to get married in the third week of September. With Arnold Jewish, and Annie Catholic, they wanted the wedding performed by a judge. They had the ceremony on the muster deck of the Police Academy on a spectacular Sunday afternoon.

Melvin and Sarah Levine attended the wedding. Ann's mother and siblings refused to attend, because they did not approve of her marring a Jewish man. They were just such insufferable, lace curtain Irish snobs. Three or four generations before, they would have been the ones being looked down on. Their absence was no loss. For the non-Gaelic, the phrase *lace curtain Irish* is not a term of endearment. It is used in a derogatory manner to describe wealthy Irish-Americans who have forgotten their roots and the struggles endured by their much poorer Irish ancestors in America. They were often just as small minded and bigoted as the people who held the Irish down for so long.

The best man was Wayne Harrison, Arnold's partner, who taught him to be a good patrol cop. The maid of honor was Ann's long time friend, Maureen Murphy.

In attendance also, were the Schnauzer and his wife, Doris, Freddie Zarullo, my wife, Mary Ann and I, the McInerney's, Sgt. Byrne, Sean Dennihy, Mr. & Mrs. Wizard, Jack Van Pelt, Danny Della Donna, Jack The Jew, Victor Velez, Sabu, Teen Angel, and Captain and Mrs. Fitzgerald.

The ceremony went off beautifully. The reception was at La Strada East. While not a banquet hall, the owner rearranged the tables and made comfortable seating for all. I felt badly for Annie Walsh, since she had no relatives attending. But, as the Book of Cynical Proverbs says "You can choose your friends, but not your relatives."

Arnold tearfully embraced his parents. He realized that it was wrong to have held a grudge for so long a time, and his parents did, too. All they had in life was each other, and they lost fifteen good years that they could never get back. All Sarah Levine wanted in life was to be was a grandmother.

Sara would soon get her wish. Arnold had been banging Annie like a screen door in a hurricane, and she was pregnant.

THE BOYS OF SUMMER

In early September Chester Podolsky was the first one of the "layoff cops" to get the phone call from his old command, asking him to return to the Aviation Unit as a helicopter pilot. Chester politely declined the offer, telling Lieutenant O'Connor that he liked the 13th Pct. and wanted to stay there.

At first, Lt. O'Connor was incredulous, saying "Chester, you've gotta be shitting me. You can come back here as a pilot. Right now, you're out on the street playing fucking cop. Aviation is a very prestigious command."

Then, O'Connor got downright nasty, threatening Chester, by saying that he could have him transferred back, against his wishes. "What the problem, Chester? What's the real reason that you won't come back?"

Having nothing to lose, since he was already on patrol, Podolsky unloaded. "Loo, when I worked for you, if I had some personal business or a family function to attend, I had to kiss your fucking ass, just to take a day off. Now, I just fill out a piece of paper and take the day off, and I don't have to kiss anybody's ass. And, there's no chicken-shit here, either. So, you can get someone else to fly your chopper. And while you're at it, you can stick your prestige where the sun doesn't shine."

Next to get the call to return was Chester's partner, Henry Mulligan. He refused to go back to the Harbor Precinct, and stayed in the 13th Pct. until the end of his career.

Sean Dennihy would not go back to Highway Patrol One, and Vinny Quaranta did not return to Public Morals. Malloy was asked to go back to the Youth Division, and crudely told his old boss to "take your Youth Division job and shove it."

The Building Maintenance Section wanted Mr. Wizard back badly, and he would not return. The fools who put him back on patrol were now spending tens of thousands of dollars in electricians' fees for work that he used to do. Van Pelt told the Emergency Service Division that he was staying put in the 13th.

Although their careers had been derailed, or destroyed, all of these men stayed on patrol for various reasons. But, most of all, it was because of the camaraderie and friendships they made over the summer that kept most of them there. They were treated like responsible men, and acted accordingly. And, most of all, there was no petty, demoralizing discipline.

One night in the Anawanda Club, Terry Malloy summed it up best, when he blurted out "This precinct is Camelot!"

After that, Aidan McSorley had a record of Richard Burton singing *Camelot* installed in the juke box. The bartender would reflexively play it whenever a member of the 13th Precinct came in. Soon, the 13th Precinct came to be known in Manhattan South as *Camelot*. The Boys of Summer were staying put in Camelot, and they would not be going anywhere for a long, long while.

CHIEF VAN DER STEIG WINS
ROUND TWO

Given the circumstances behind our abrupt transfers, Tommy and I would not be getting any phone calls to return to our former details any time soon, certainly not in this decade. Round One of the battle between Van Der Steig and Fitzgerald had gone to the Captain on points, but the Chief would not be denied, with his anal, petty, vindictive, personal crusade against Captain Fitz.

Van Der Steig also knew how to play the game, and did not give up in his scheme to publicly dump Fitzgerald. In reviewing the 13th Precinct statistics, the Chief noted that crime was down in every category. However, there were fewer parking tickets given out so far in 1975, compared to the same period of 1974. Overlooking the fact that some five thousand cops had been laid off, perhaps the remaining men were too busy answering the public's calls for help and arresting criminals, than to ticket for an expired parking meter.

In the NYPD there is an irrational urge to equate the department's success with numbers. Basically, if your precinct gave out 2,000 parking tickets or red light summonses in one year, you had to give out more the next year. Of course, why would they ever consider the fact that you had fewer police officers, and the public may be engaging in more voluntary compliance? A rational person would look at it that way, but not the NYPD leadership.

Reliance on numbers as a measure of success of the police mission is the crutch of the dim-witted, incompetent, unimaginative police commander. In theory, the purpose of giving out summonses is to achieve voluntary compliance with the law. However, it has deteriorated into a revenue generating scam for the City of New

York, with the higher-ups complicit in the self-destructive debacle. Once the public starts complying with the law, the police should then back off and leave them alone, lest they be seen as an oppressive force, rather than a helping hand.

Somehow, the police brass cannot see this, and continue to order more summonses given out to a more compliant, law-abiding population. The public resentment caused by this over-enforcement damages the reputation of the police department. People who have received petty, picayune summonses, and lost a day's pay because some cop needed a *number*, are not going to cooperate with the police in other things, like providing information about criminals. This logic is lost on those in charge at One Police Plaza, many of whom lack actual patrol experience.

The nitwit, numbers-driven mentality of the NYPD brass was, and is, a public relations disaster, and one that would never be tolerated in private industry. No corporation or business entity would ever want to ruin its own reputation for honesty and fair dealing with the public. However, the high command of the NYPD continues to engage in this idiotic, self-destructive behavior, to this day.

So it was with Chief Willem Van Der Steig. In 1975, the 13th Pct. had given out about 300 fewer parking tickets that the year before. Now, Van Der Steig found a pretext to remove the Precinct C.O. It did not help Captain Fitzgerald's cause to have publicly criticized the mayor and Police Commissioner in harsh, unflattering language for the layoff of Police Officers, while the City of New York had over a million and half welfare recipients on the dole, and city officials kept luring more and more of them to move here.

In the NYPD there are few secrets, and Captain Fitzgerald got wind that he was about to get sacked. He would not give the prick Van Der Steig the delight of publicly removing him, and he abruptly put in his retirement papers.

The announcement of our C.O.'s retirement came as a shock

to the men of the 13th Pct. He was more of a revered father figure than a commander. Everyone suspected, correctly, that Van Der Steig's fingerprints were all over this. The union delegates spread the word that our Captain got fired over a lack of parking tickets. The cops were told not to issue any summonses, unless they really had to.

The Chief was about to get a real stern lesson in *numbers*. Like, *zero* is a number. Any cop who gave out a summons that was not absolutely necessary would have his locker turned upside down and put in the shower for a few hours.

ROOFTOP RESCUE

In police work, if you let your guard down, even for an instant, it can prove fatal. On patrol, whether you're in a big city or small town, you have to keep your shit together and your ass wired tight at all times. Even a veteran cop can make a mistake that could end his life in an instant. I would soon find this out the hard way.

Life was gritty in the tenements of 24th to 30th Streets, between First to Third Avenues. Most of the buildings were pre- World War II, five story walk-ups, and had a mixture of working class, poverty cases, snotty yuppies, and no shortage of criminals. Crime was a fact of life in these tenements.

The quiet evening about 11:00 P.M. was interrupted by the dispatcher assigning us to a job: "Female calls for help, on the roof. Caller states that it is between 322 and 332 East 29th Streets. No further information."

We took off and got there in less than a minute... Tommy went to no. 322 and I went to no. 332. We agreed to check out the roof tops and work our way toward each other. In Manhattan the rooftops are dark at night, and most of the light from below fails to reach there, as well as street noise, so you work in near total, silent darkness. In addition, some landlords painted over the old skylights with black paint or tar, so you had to be careful where you walked, or you could fall to your death five stories below to the lobby.

I made my way up to the top of the building, two steps at a time. Opening the door, I stepped out of the bulkhead onto the roof, only to face an eerie stillness, and the blackness of a typical Manhattan rooftop. I looked around cautiously, but saw and heard nothing. The Empire State Building looked so close to me that it seemed like I could just reach out and touch it.

Maybe this was a prank call. It was then that I made a foolish mistake that nearly cost me my life. When alone on a rooftop, a cop should never stand near the edge of the roof. You could be easily pushed off by a criminal or a psycho. Even though I knew that, my complacency led me to kneel down and peer over the two foot high red brick parapet, and looked over the side of the building for someone on the nearby fire escape.

I heard footsteps coming toward me. Not wanting to panic, I convinced myself that it was just my partner coming closer. But why would Tommy be running? I slowly turned half around and was horrified to see a tall, well-built man about five feet from me, and closing fast. He dove at me like I was a tackling dummy, trying to push me off of the roof. I was now turned, facing him, and in an instant I had half of my body hanging over the roof, while my attacker kept pushing me to my certain death in the garbage strewn courtyard, fifty feet below.

I had decent upper body strength, but this man was much more powerful than me. All I could do was hold onto him and try to get more of my body back onto the roof. By the grace of God my gun belt became stuck on the sharp edge of the bricks, and for the time being it kept me from sliding off any further.

My dilemma was that if I let go of my opponent with my right hand and went for my gun, I would lose the battle and would be flipped over the edge to my death before I could shoot him. Where the hell was my partner?

I began to get that sickening feeling in my gut that it was all over for me, and thought about my son or daughter who would grow up without their father, because I made a dumb mistake on some dark rooftop, on a long ago forgotten summer night in Manhattan in the summer of '75.

Just when I thought I was seconds from death, a shadowy figure appeared behind the man who was trying to kill me. I had heard stories about the Angel of Death. Was this him actually coming for me?

Miraculously, it was Brian Conner from sector Charlie-David, who heard the call and decided to back us up. Conner hauled off and hit my attacker a shot across the head, which only stunned the man. Merely annoyed, he released his death grip on me for the moment. Brian then used his nightstick to put a choke hold on him.

I was able to break free and got to my feet. The 150 pound Conner was too small to maintain the choke hold on the 250 pound man. Just as my attacker flung Brian off of him like he was a rag doll, I kicked him right in the groin, making him bend over at the waist. I picked up Conner's nightstick and, in blind rage, began to beat my would-be killer with blows to his arms, shoulders and shins until the man could no longer put up a fight. He fell to the kneeling position, unable to lift up his arms due to the beating.

With all of my remaining strength, I pulled his head toward me, and kneed him right in the jaw, knocking him unconscious for a few minutes. I was insane with rage.

"Try to kill me, you worthless piece of shit? Make my wife a fucking widow? I'll kill you, you fucking bastard!"

For a brief moment, I entertained the idea of throwing this bum off of the roof, but quickly came to my senses.

My savior was hurt and bleeding badly; I was hyperventilating so much that I thought that I was going to pass out. McInerney and Mazzarella soon came running to our aid. I was too exhausted to cuff the prisoner, so Tommy did it for me.

It turned out that the man who tried to kill me was named Calvin Lounds. He had done time for rape twice, and was on parole. This night he had taken a young girl up to the roof and tried to rape her, but she screamed for help. He beat her until she was unconscious. Tommy found her a few buildings away and called for an ambulance.

This was it for Lounds. He faced a new charge of attempted

rape, plus attempted murder of a police officer. This dangerous man would now get life imprisonment as a three time loser.

Brian Conner hit the side of his head on a jagged vent pipe and had a nasty gash that needed more than thirty stitches to close, and to also sew his ear back together. He received a tetanus shot, to boot.

About an hour and a half later Conner returned to the station house and received a hero's welcome for saving a fellow cop from certain death.

I approached Brian in the muster room, and with a serious face said "If I ever want a fucking back-up, I'll call for a fucking back-up." Then both of us cracked up laughing, and I embraced him tightly for giving me the rest of my life back.

"Now we're even, Jimmy", Brian said.

In just a few weeks the Precinct had turned around one hundred eighty degrees and became a great place to work. Now the cops felt a sense of loyalty and brotherhood to each other. This was the NYPD I knew and loved.

I lay in bed in the station house dorm that night, but even with five beers under my belt, I could not sleep. Tossing, turning, and sweating profusely, I kept thinking over and over "How could I have made such a stupid, rookie mistake?"

Having narrowly escaped death again my nervous system was shot, and I wondered why I was still on this job that paid so little, and caused so much anguish. I knew the answer in my heart. 'The Job' was in my blood, and once having experienced the adrenaline rush of real police work, and the camaraderie of good, solid men, I could do nothing else in life and enjoy it.

But, many years later, I still recalled the eerie words that an old timer said to me my first week on patrol. "Don't love 'The Job', kid. The Job is a whore, and she won't love you back."

BACK SEAT BUGGERY

Two days later, I downed my last beer at the Anawanda and called it a night about 1:00 A.M. Heading along East 20th Street toward the F.D.R. Drive, I realized that I should have taken a leak before I left the bar. There was no way I could hold in those beers all the way to Staten Island.

The area along the East River between E. 16th Street to E. 20th Street was desolate, with an old cement factory being the only building around. I parked my car in a vacant lot that had about two dozen cars in it, and looked for an obscure spot inside the abandoned building to relieve myself. On the way back to my auto, I looked around and saw a familiar car about forty or fifty feet away. It was a maroon 1969 Chevy, with distinctive white pin striping, and it looked just like Sean Dennihy's car. I walked closer and peered in the rear window. There was Sean in the back seat, with his pants around his knees. He was with a blond woman and he was banging her in the doggie position. Her blouse was unbuttoned to expose two huge breasts, and her skirt was up over her hips.

I said to myself as I walked back to my car, "Good for him. Looks like Sean's got a girlfriend and forgotten his personal problems for the time being."

When I got back to my car I had to brush off the cement dust from my shoes. Heading south on Avenue C, I saw the interior light to Sean's car go on, and giving in to perverse curiosity, I slowed down to see what his girlfriend looked like. What I saw next shocked, stunned and upset me. Laverne, the transvestite who lived next door to the Precinct, exited the car smoking a cigarette and buttoning her blouse. I was in total shock and disbelief at this point, and sped off to avoid being seen.

My gut was queasy, and I was in a state of mental confusion, not believing, nor wanting to believe what I had just seen. I drove past the entrance to the F.D.R. Drive, pulled over, and vomited my guts out all over the street. For fifteen minutes I sat on the front bumper of my beat up green Volkswagen, staring down at the puddle of my beer-soaked puke and half digested egg roll, much like a dazed shaman trying to read tea leaves.

Desperately trying to understand what I had just witnessed, I was in a state of denial.

When I regained my composure a bit I headed back home. At age twenty-nine I thought that I had seen it all and knew it all, and was certainly no naïve kid. However, seeing my friend Sean Dennihy buggering that transvestite was something that I found hard to believe, but I was mature enough to know that I had to, bitter as it was to accept. But, sweet Jeezus, I had just seen Sean Dennihy corn-holing Laverne. Mother-fucking Laverne!

I tried to see the bright side of this by rationalizing that maybe Sean didn't know, or maybe he was drunk and just fell in love with her tits. Then I thought that, at least he was the pitcher, and not the catcher. But still, all I could say to myself, over and over, all the way home was "What the fuck! What the fuck!"

What else could occur this summer that would forever change the way I saw life? How much more jaded, hardened, and cynical could I become?

What the fuck, indeed!!!

LOOKING BACK

As the summer came to a close, I began to look at my life as I had never done before. I had once been a confident, cocky guy, with no worries, but now I was entering into the uncharted waters of fatherhood. For the first time in my life I was on the balls of my ass, in the economic sense. With inflation, and having had our pay cut, I was more broke than I had ever been. I was never rich, but prior to this, I always had some money in my pocket. To further destroy us, the mayor took away our free transit, so now we had to pay on the subway, *and* fight every punk on the train and ferry who acted up and caused a problem.

In addition to being a process server for Jerry Callahan, I also worked on the side for Harry Holzer, a detective in the Ballistics Section of the Lab. Harry had an exterminating business on the side, and had so much work he could not handle it by himself. Harry had a strict work ethic, and he maintained his side business just like he was when he was a patrol cop with me back in the West Village. He was a perfectionist and a stickler for detail. On many days, I would get up at 8:00 A.M. and work for Harry until 1:00 P.M. Then, I would shower to try to get the chlordane smell from my skin, and manage to show up at the Precinct at 4:00 P.M. It was difficult work, but I had to do it, just to keep my modest house from going into foreclosure.

With my wife expecting in March or April of 1976, I had to earn some money. I had a whopping $1,000.00 in the bank, and even with insurance, the doctor and incidentals would be another $500.00. Tommy and I wondered what was wrong with the people running New York City. They could not pay their police, but continued to lure welfare recipients to come here and live off the dwindling base of taxpayers. It was nothing short of insanity. For the politicians, there was a lot of money to be made in poverty.

When some liberal relative would defend the welfare recipients, repeating the old canard "They really want to work, but they just can't find jobs", I used to say, "Yeah, that's because I have three of them!"

I asked myself many times over the summer "A few months ago, I was a happy-go-lucky guy. How did I get so screwed-up in such a short time?" I realized that I was slowly being worn down by the grinding weight of the poverty of the working poor, i.e. those making too much to qualify for government benefits, yet earning too little to enjoy life. It was a bitter feeling that would stay with me throughout my entire life.

BEN COMES HOME

Ben Harrigan was released from Sloan Kettering in mid-September. His full head of black hair was gone, but was beginning to grow back. He had undergone eight weeks of chemotherapy, but was in full remission now. Seeing him at his Brooklyn apartment with his mother, Kathleen, we had a tearful reunion. They were very grateful for what the Precinct had done. All I wanted was for Ben to be restored to good health. Since I was frustrated in my inability to save my own brother, I was happy that Ben was saved.

HARD LESSONS LEARNED

Despite the financial problems of the City of New York, and the Kavanaugh household, I still thought that it was a great time to be alive. In the summer of '75, I had never been more broke, nor had more laughs in my whole life. It brought to mind the words of Charles Dickens: *It was the best of times, it was the worst of times.*

Having been roughed up over the past summer, both emotionally and financially, these tough life experiences made me a different person. From all the troubles and hardships that I endured, I became a much better man, even considering the state of financial embarrassment in which I found myself. Since coming to the 13th Precinct I learned many valuable lessons from the people I worked with, from those I encountered on patrol, from Father Higgins, and from life in general. Most importantly, I wasn't such a *know it all* any more, and learned to be a better listener, realizing that someone else's ideas and problems were just as important to them as mine were to me. Sometimes, all you need to do to help someone is to just be a good listener, even if you can't do anything to resolve their problem.

Sitting with my partner at the Anawanda Club on a mid-September afternoon, we two barstool philosophers began to recall the events of the past summer. I was expounding on how all of my experiences changed me as a man, as a cop, and how I saw life in general. Tommy was not into such touch-feely stuff, but he listened attentively, as any good friend and partner would.

Captain Fitzgerald, Lt. Cantorwicz, and Sgt. Byrne brought out the fact that a good boss does not have to be a mean-spirited man, a screamer, nor nasty or cruel to get the job done. You can get

253

people to work for you by treating them with dignity and respect. I would remember the meaning of *noblesse oblige* in later years when I became a Sergeant and a Lieutenant.

Saying nothing to my partner, I looked back at how Sean Dennihy handled his marital problems with graciousness and class. I now knew what Father Higgins meant by forgiving those who have hurt you along life's way, and the harmful effect of holding grudges.

The self-destructive behavior of holding grudges against family members was brought out by the Levines. The three of them had only each other in life, but they lost fifteen valuable years that they could never get back.

I would never forget Mr. and Mrs. Kowalski, and how they unselfishly sacrificed their own lives to help their handicapped son for over fifty years. What great people they were.

I remembered the first time I had seen Annie Walsh in her Auxiliary Police uniform, with the ugly, metal braces on her legs. My mistake was in smugly dismissing her as just a *wanabee* cop with crippled legs, instead of looking at the whole person, as Arnold had done. From now on, whenever I met a disfigured, handicapped, or a person with special needs, I now knew enough to look past their condition and speak to the person inside of them who was talking to me.

As personally tortured as I was over losing my brother Frank to mental illness, I took Father Charlie's advice that you can't blame God for every negative thing that happens in your life. You have to accept the truth from the Book of Cynical Proverbs which states that "Sometimes, bad things happen to good people." You have to move on with your life, and pray that God will give your afflicted family member a better life in the next world. In fact, most families have at least one hurtful, gut wrenching issue that tears at their souls. Maybe it's an untimely death, a crippling injury, a suicide, drug abuse, mental problems of a loved one, or a divorce.

Even the worst individuals like Sergeants Hanley, Nordstrom

and McNally can have some positive benefit. They could always serve as a bad example to their subordinates on how not to be a leader.

Johnny Byrne proved to be a great role model for me. Byrne was a good man, who led by example. In later years I would have the privilege of working with him when we were both Lieutenants.

Among the many things I experienced from working with my great partner, Tommy McInerney, was not to take myself too seriously and be able to laugh at myself now and then, especially whenever I screwed up. Most importantly, I appreciated how valuable a good, reliable, honest partner is to a cop.

Al Jackson, having been treated badly by the department, continued to serve the City of New York with great dedication, never whining or complaining.

He showed me how to take life's beatings, defeats, and setbacks, and wear them like a soldier wears a Purple Heart.

From all of the subway *jumpers* who threw themselves under the train, the anguish of Ben's illness, seeing Sgt. Lawless in his last days, the kid from the Kenmore Hotel, and Uncle Carl's sudden death, we realized that in life, good health is always more important than money (although it's pretty damn good to have money, too, as we were finding out).

Thinking of my pregnant wife, I learned not to take the love of a good woman for granted. I loved my wife even more as we awaited the birth of our first child.

Although we were humbled and exhausted by our side jobs, both of us still felt that there was dignity in all work, and a lack of it in being a career welfare recipient.

Looking back at Capt. Fitzgerald, Lt. Cantorwicz, Billy Burke, Numb Nuts Noonan, and their peers, I saw them as truly being the greatest generation of Americans. World War II veterans were great men and women who put their country ahead of their personal ambitions, while asking for nothing in return.

In civil service jobs, you get paid every other Thursday whether you work hard or not. After working for Jerry Callahan for three months, I now understood how hard the self-employed have to work just to make a buck. At the end of the week they don't stick out their hand and get a check. The self-employed have to hustle to earn a living. I had a much greater respect for them now.

Although the legal profession had some bottom-feeders like Schmucklein and Judge Levitt, it was attorneys like Weinberg and Callahan who exemplified what the true role of lawyers in society is all about. You can never appreciate the real value of an attorney until you have been wrongfully accused of a crime and he comes to your defense. After the police, attorneys are a civilized society's second line of defense.

Numb Nuts Noonan's experience drove home the old adage that if you stay in police work too long, nothing good is going to happen to you.

I felt great sympathy for Al Hodge, my old Captain Video, a good, yet imperfect man. Fame and fortune are fleeting, and can be easily lost, but dignity and class stay with a man forever. How the imprudent use of liquor can destroy even the best of men! Upon seeing Mr. Hodge fall into alcoholism, I knew that I had to reduce my own consumption of beer, which had become excessive.

The mentally ill are treated cruelly in our society. I never gave them much attention until Frank was stricken with schizophrenia. They are easily mocked, mimicked, and ridiculed, and they are seldom understood. In my ignorance, I had been guilty of this. Civil rights advocates believed that it was a wonderful thing to dump these poor unfortunates back onto the streets, rather than treating them in hospitals or clinics. They prided themselves on bringing court cases which would put people like Frank out to live on their own, with no medication or psychiatric care, only to be beaten, and robbed of their money, and what little dignity they had. Now I had a deeper understanding of mental illness. The A.C.L.U. and their ilk, along with the left wing, activist judges who support them, should be damned to hell for what they have done to the mentally ill in America.

Tommy and I discussed our run-in with the whining limey, Wellington Hartshorne. I thought a lot about what I had told him, then realized that the oath I took many years ago when I came on the job was more important.

If I failed to help the people I was sworn to protect, I wouldn't be much of a cop, even in the face of phony complaints. We rationalized that civilian complaints were just part of the job, and you can't let them prevent you from keeping the streets safe. For the rest of my career, I would continue to battle the criminals, junkies, and their worthless ilk, and take my lumps from the cop-hating political hacks in the Civilian Complaint Review Board.

I would never forget the incredible shock I experienced upon seeing my friend, Sean Dennihy, having a sexual relationship with a transvestite. I learned to accept it, and still thought highly of Sean. But, you can never, ever fathom the demons that are raging in another man's head. I never revealed to anyone what I had witnessed Sean doing, and kept it to myself. As I matured over this most difficult summer of my life, I learned to channel my rigid, myopic cynicism into a healthy skepticism.

My brushes with death were a great reminder of the value of life, and from then on I tried to live every day like it could be my last.

Despite all of the problems with our low pay and poor working conditions, I still felt that the NYPD was the greatest job in the world. As I said many times before "I had a front row seat to the greatest show in the world."

Most importantly, I came to the realization that no matter how tough you are, you can't go down the difficult road of life on your own. Sooner or later, everyone will need God in their life as their back-up.

EPILOGUE

The residents of New York City did not realize how close they came to disaster by the layoff of thousands of police officers. It was only due to the dedication and sacrifice of the older members of the NYPD that the City of New York was kept safe, held together, and survived. They had their careers destroyed, delayed and derailed, yet were a great group of loyal, dedicated cops.

New York City's political leaders were so incompetent and out of control that eventually the city's financial affairs had to be taken over by a group of responsible adults, called the Financial Control Board.

It took the firm hand and no-nonsense leadership of Mayor Edward I. Koch to restore the City of New York to fiscal and social sanity. Mayor Koch was a World War II infantry Sergeant who described himself as "a liberal with sanity." New York City cops never had a better friend than this greatest of men, Mayor Ed Koch, nor has our city ever had a better mayor.

Thank you for saving our city, Mr. Mayor!

About the Author

James J. Kavanaugh (a pseudonym) is a retired Lieutenant from the New York City Police Department. He served in the NYPD from 1964 to 1987, leaving for two years to serve in the United States Army during the Vietnam War. In the Army he was a member of the Military Police Corps. During his tenure in the NYPD, Kavanaugh worked as a patrol officer in Manhattan's Greenwich Village, and in the Gramercy Park Precinct. He also served as an instructor in the Police Academy.

After being promoted to Sergeant, Kavanaugh served as a patrol supervisor in Brooklyn. Promoted to Lieutenant in 1983, he worked in Police Headquarters and the Police Academy. The author holds B.S. and M.A. degrees from John Jay College of Criminal Justice, and a Juris Doctor degree from Brooklyn Law School.

At the present time, Mr. Kavanaugh is an attorney in New York City.

LaVergne, TN USA
06 January 2011
211233LV00005B/142/P